D0679865

Zelensky: A Biography

ZELENSKY
A Biography

SERHII RUDENKO

Translated by
Michael M. Naydan and Alla Perminova

polity

Originally published in Ukrainian as *Зеленський без гриму* in 2021
© Serhii Rudenko. Agreement via Wiedling Literary Agency.

This English edition © Polity Press, 2022

Polity Press
65 Bridge Street
Cambridge CB2 1UR, UK

Polity Press
111 River Street
Hoboken, NJ 07030, USA

ISBN-13: 978-1-5095-5638-0

A catalogue record for this book is available from the British Library.

Library of Congress Control Number 2022939916

Typeset in 11.5 on 14.5pt Warnock Pro
by Cheshire Typesetting Ltd, Cuddington, Cheshire

The publisher has used its best endeavours to ensure that the URLs for
external websites referred to in this book are correct and active at the
time of going to press. However, the publisher has no responsibility for
the websites and can make no guarantee that a site will remain live or that
the content is or will remain appropriate.

Every effort has been made to trace all copyright holders, but if any have
been overlooked the publisher will be pleased to include any necessary
credits in any subsequent reprint or edition.

For further information on Polity, visit our website:
politybooks.com

Contents

Abbreviations

ATO (Anti-Terrorist Operation)
BPP (Petro Poroshenko Bloc)
BRDO (Better Regulation Delivery Office)
CJSC (Closed Joint-Stock Company)
CPSU (Communist Party of the Soviet Union)
CPU (Communist Party of Ukraine)
DBR (State Bureau of Investigation)
DPI (Donetsk Polytechnic Institute)
DPR (Donetsk People's Republic)
HPU (Office of the Prosecutor General)
HUR MO (Chief Office of Intelligence of the Ministry of Defense)
KVK (Club of the Cheerful and Quick-Witted – Ukrainian)
KVN (Club of the Cheerful and Quick-Witted – Russian)
LKSMU (Leninist Communist Union of Ukrainian Youth)
LPR (Luhansk People's Republic)
NABU (National Anti-Corruption Bureau of Ukraine)
NAZK (National Agency on Corruption Prevention)
NBU (National Bank of Ukraine)
NSK (National Sports Complex)

ODA (Regional State Administration)
ORDLO (the temporarily occupied territory of Ukraine)
OSCE (Organization for Security and Cooperation in
     Europe)
PVK (Private Military Company)
RNBO (National Security and Defense Council)
SAP (Anti-Corruption Prosecutor's Office)
SBU (Security Service of Ukraine)
SDPU(o) (Social Democratic Party of Ukraine (united))
SZR (Foreign Intelligence Service)
TCG (Trilateral Contact Group)
TsBK (Central Election Commission)

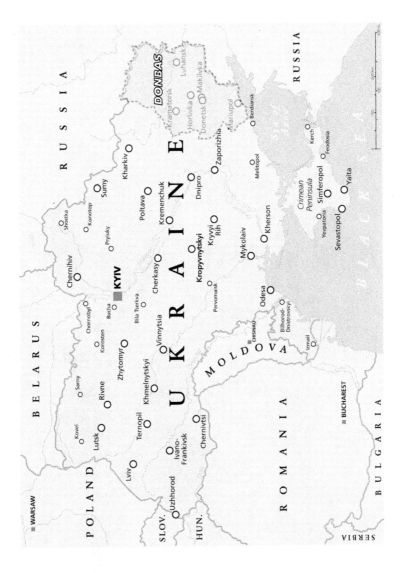

Preface

Zelensky's Political Oscar

On April 21, 2019, at 8:00 p.m., Volodymyr Zelensky and members of his team appeared before journalists to the sounds of the song "I Love My Country" from the soundtrack to the film (and TV series) *Servant of the People*.

At that moment, it seemed that this simple song was being sung not only by the victorious candidate himself, but also by the 73 percent of the electorate who had voted for him.

Ukrainian and foreign journalists, who flooded the capital's Parkovy Convention and Exhibition Center, were looking forward to the victory speech of the newly elected president. Zelensky was radiant. And so were those who had led him to victory: Andriy Bohdan, Dmytro Razumkov, Kyrylo Tymoshenko, Andriy Yermak, Oleksandr Danyliuk, and Zelensky's wife Olena. Confetti was flying all around them, the hall was buzzing, the staff were ready to dance for joy.

"We did it together . . . ," Zelensky began his speech, with his characteristic intonation. First, as befits an actor at the

Oscars, he thanked his team, family, relatives, his wife Olena, and even two cleaning ladies, Oksana and Lyuba, who kept the headquarters neat and tidy. He also mentioned the symbolic 73rd section at the Olympic Stadium, where he and his team shot the famous video *Stadion tak Stadion* ("Let It Be the Stadium Then!").

Zelensky was still in the character of Vasyl Holoborodko – the protagonist of the film and TV series – and tried to joke, to toss barbs at the SBU (Security Service of Ukraine), which, according to him, kept him on his toes at all times, and to show optimism. It seems that, in saying goodbye to his acting career, Zelensky was counting on the same raucous applause as he entered the political arena. Sure enough, he was used to being loved by the public and to hearing shouts of "Bravo" and "Encore!" It was no small wonder. He had received ovations in grand concert halls and theaters in Moscow, Kyiv, Odesa, Jurmala, Minsk, and other cities of the former Soviet Union; he became a rising star in 1997 after appearing in Aleksandr Maslyakov's game show *KVN* (Club of the Cheerful and Quick-Witted).[1] This was when television fame anointed the 19-year-old actor. Prior to his presidency, Volodymyr Zelensky was a popular actor beloved by many Ukrainians.

But, on the evening of April 21, 2019, having won a landslide victory in the presidential election, could he have imagined that, only about six months later, he would, after addressing a crowd, be hearing: "Shame!" and "Away with Zelya!"?[2] And not only from the supporters of his main opponent Petro Poroshenko, but also from volunteers, the military, and politicians.

---

[1] A competitive comedy skit game show *Klub veselykh i nakhodchivykh* filmed in Moscow.
[2] Pejorative nickname for Zelensky.

A few months after the inauguration, Zelensky started dismissing those who had led him to victory. The first to go was the secretary of the RNBO (National Security and Defense Council) Oleksandr Danyliuk, who allegedly took offense at Zelensky for not making him prime minister. The second member to leave the team was the head of the Office of the President Andriy Bohdan, who had been with him since his first steps in bigtime politics. Then, Prime Minister Oleksiy Honcharuk and Prosecutor General Ruslan Ryaboshapka both lost their posts.

All these people were part of the Zelensky collective, elected by the country on April 21, 2019. Because right through to the end of the presidential campaign there was no such thing as Zelensky the politician. At all. He was a talented comedian, manager of the Inter TV channel and Kvartal 95 Studio. An actor who played the high-school teacher Vasyl Holoborodko, who, in the TV series, became head of state. Zelensky's presidential image was constructed by those around him.

In 2019, Ukraine's sixth president announced: "I promise I will never let you all down." Since then, we have seen Zelensky in various situations. He and his team have been criticized for being unprofessional. They have been accused of corruption, arrogance, and even treason. However, starting from February 24, 2022, the beginning of Russia's large-scale invasion of the Ukrainian state, we have discovered a completely different Zelensky. A man who was not afraid to accept Putin's challenge and become the leader of popular resistance to Russian aggression. A president who managed to unite in this fight his supporters and opponents, corrupt officials and fighters against corruption, adults and children, people of different nationalities and faiths. A head of state who is greeted with applause in European parliaments and the US Congress.

Each episode in the life of the sixth president of Ukraine as presented in this book forms a piece in the mosaic of the portrait of Volodymyr Zelensky. A man who, without political experience and relevant knowledge, promised Ukrainians he would change the state. A man trusted by 13.5 million voters.

There will be no moralizing, prejudice, or manipulation in this book. Just facts. I will try to recreate the portrait of the sixth president of Ukraine devoid of actor's greasepaint.

How successful I have been will be for you, kind readers, to judge.

Episode 1

Ten Assassination Attempts on President Zelensky

On February 24, 2022, at 4:50 a.m., Russia launched the first missile strikes on Ukrainian territory. At the same time as Russian television was broadcasting Vladimir Putin's address to his people, the first ballistic missiles were falling on Ukrainians in their capital city Kyiv, as well as in Kharkiv, Odesa, Mariupol, Dnipro, and other cities. A few kilometers from my house in Kyiv, in Brovary and Boryspil, the ground shook with explosions. Sleepy cities were recovering from the first shock. Sirens of ambulances, fire engines, and rescue vehicles pierced the winter air. My conscious mind refused to accept the fact that Russia was bombing a free and independent state in the center of Europe. It seemed like a nightmare that might end with the first rays of the sun.

However, this was not a bad dream. It was a new reality into which Ukrainians had awakened.

An hour and a half after the first strikes, Zelensky addressed the people and confirmed the beginning of the Russian war against Ukraine. And as dawn broke, news emerged about the first victims of the Kremlin's attack — those who were at military sites hit by missiles. Thus the large-scale invasion of Ukraine by the Russian Federation began, something no one wanted to believe until the very last moment. This included Volodymyr Zelensky. A month before the war, despite warnings from American and British intelligence about a possible Russian attack, the president insisted that everything was under his complete control and that foreigners were simply spreading unjustified panic.

During the night of February 24, just a few hours before the war began, the Ukrainian president publicly addressed the Russians. He sincerely hoped he could stop Putin – even though, after the annexation of Crimea and the occupation of part of the Donbas in 2014, it was clear that the master of the Kremlin could only be stopped by the complete surrender of Ukraine or by a bullet in his forehead. Putin tried to convince everyone that Ukrainian statehood began with Vladimir Lenin, and that Ukrainians were a people invented by Count Potocki. Incidentally, he repeated this before the attack on Ukraine, despite the fact that the Ukrainian capital was founded when the site of modern Moscow consisted of nothing but swampland. Putin's public desire to defend the so-called "independence" of the pseudo-republics of the LPR (Luhansk People's Republic) and the DPR (Donetsk People's Republic) was the only reason given for his attempt to destroy the Ukrainian state.

President Zelensky faced Putin's challenge with dignity. Despite numerous proposals from the United States and ten assassination attempts (this at least was the number indicated in March by Mykhailo Podoliak, an advisor to the Office of the President), he did not abandon Kyiv. Putin wanted Zelensky dead, if not physically, then at least politically. And the fact that this did not happen shows the weakness of the master of the Kremlin. Zelensky's office in the center of the Ukrainian capital has become one of the important symbols of the invincibility of the Ukrainian people. The unembellished courage with which he, as the Supreme Commander-in-Chief of the Armed Forces of Ukraine, entered the war with Russia truly impressed Ukrainians, and in particular his opponents. He received standing ovations in European parliaments and became the center of world attention. Volodymyr Zelensky's current popularity in the West can only be compared to that of former Soviet President Mikhail Gorbachev.

The blitzkrieg that Vladimir Putin was counting on in Ukraine failed. Russia encountered fierce resistance from the Ukrainian people, led by Zelensky. The Kremlin seemed unprepared for the fact that the war unleashed by Russia would be seen as a real war by the Ukrainian people. The Russian aggressors were met with fire – not only from the military, but also from ordinary citizens. For the first time in Ukraine's recent history, we have seen the people unite against an external enemy.

In time, historians will no doubt write about Zelensky's role and his victory in the Russo-Ukrainian war. Films will be made and books will be written about him; streets, avenues, and universities will be named after him. Zelensky will be associated with the period in Ukrainian history that will be called "the final rupture between Ukraine and Russia."

For centuries, Ukrainians have fought against Moscow for the right to be free and independent. Millions of people sacrificed their lives in bloody resistance. It seemed that there would be no end to the wars between Ukrainians and Russia. Until recently, the Kremlin had hoped to be able to keep Ukraine in its orbit. And its miscalculation stems from just this. Vladimir Putin, in particular, got it wrong when he spoke disparagingly about Volodymyr Zelensky. Ironically, the one person whom the Russian president refused to accept as an equal has become the undertaker of the modern Russian regime.

Episode 2

The Campaign for President

It's December 31, 2018. Five minutes to midnight.

Ukrainians are about to see in the New Year with champagne glasses in their hands. There's the countdown, in anticipation of the president's speech. For Petro Poroshenko, this New Year's greeting is his final one as head of state.

Political science is merciless. Only 11.6 percent of the electorate, according to the Kyiv International Institute of Sociology, is ready to vote for the incumbent president. The favorite in the race is Poroshenko's longtime opponent Yuliya Tymoshenko, with a projected 21.2 percent of the vote. The third most likely presidential candidate, Volodymyr Zelensky, artistic director of Kvartal 95 Studio, with a projected 14.6 percent of the vote, has not yet said a word about his intention to run for office.

The traditional New Year's performance of Kvartal 95 on the 1+1 TV channel is interrupted for congratulations from the president. But instead of Poroshenko, Volodymyr Zelensky appears on the screen. In a white shirt with rolled up sleeves, he comes out from backstage. "Good evening, friends . . . ," he begins in Russian, and fifteen seconds later switches to Ukrainian.

He talks about three paths that Ukrainians can choose.

The first is to live as before.

The second is to pack up and go abroad.

And the third is to try to change things in Ukraine.

"And I choose the third path for myself. People have been asking me for a long time – are you running or not? You know, unlike our great politicians, I didn't want to offer you empty promises. But now, a few minutes before the New Year, I am promising you something and will do so right away. Dear Ukrainians, I'm promising you I will run for president. And I'm doing it right away. I'm running for president," Zelensky announced.

I am sure that most people sitting at their festive New Year's tables did not realize just what had happened at that moment. All this looked like part of a Kvartal 95 show.

It was like a concert backstage. Dimmed light. A smiling Zelensky. The Paddington Bear voice that he used when dubbing the cartoon movie. Well, what the hell kind of damn presidential candidate is he? Where's the tie? Where's his suit? Where are the traditional words filled with pathos? Where is all this? And where is Petro Poroshenko? Supporters of the fifth president, seeing Zelensky instead of Poroshenko on their screens, were raging on social networks. "Who? This clown?," "Who is he to run for president?," "What insolence!" Subscribers didn't hold anything back in their comments about Zelensky, the oligarch Ihor Kolomoisky who controls 1+1, and Oleksandr Tkachenko, the channel's general director, who would later become a people's deputy in the Servant of the People Party and, later, Ukraine's minister of culture.

Apparently, the statement of the artistic director of Kvartal 95 Studio was perceived as a bad joke in many election headquarters.

However, on New Year's Eve, Zelensky was more serious than ever.

Those who took the actor's performance to be a famous comedian's joke had no idea that Zelensky had already decided, a long time before, to run for president. His team had been preparing for the election for quite a while. Throughout the summer of 2018, Zelensky kept the intrigue going, trolling the popular frontman of the Okean Elzy band Svyatoslav Vakarchuk: "Slava, are you going to run or not? Because if you are, so am I. So, if your answer is an ironclad 'yes' or a definite 'no,' then so is mine. Because everyone keeps asking, well, what about me? And what about me? As far as I am concerned, everything is clear. What about you? Because if it's you and me, then it's us. Do you understand? And if it's 'we,' then – everyone."

According to the politician Roman Bezsmertny, he met with Svyatoslav Vakarchuk and asked him not to run for president and to convince Volodymyr Zelensky of the same. As Bezsmertny once told me:

> I said, "Slava, I respect you as an artist, but please meet with Zelensky and agree that neither you nor Zelensky will run. Because if you do both run, you will simply break Ukraine and it will be very difficult to know what will happen next." I don't know whether Vakarchuk listened to me or to someone else, but he acted very wisely: he did not run. Instead, he missed his chance during the parliamentary campaign. And I understand this perfectly, because I knew for sure that neither of them was able to shoulder the problems facing Ukraine, the key one being war.

Nevertheless, in fall 2018, the headquarters of the presidential candidate were formed, joined by political strategist Dmytro Razumkov – almost the only media figure at the time (other than, of course, the frontman of Kvartal 95).

Zelensky's team was preparing for the election. During the winter of 2018–19, they paid for advertising on the radio and on billboards with the slogan "I'm not kidding." It was during this period that the première of the third season of the series *Servant of the People* was postponed. In it, the current president of Ukraine played the role of the teacher Vasyl Holoborodko, who suddenly, surprising even himself, becomes president.

But hardly anyone in Zelensky's team was counting on victory then. And Zelensky himself, according to the former head of the Office of the President Andriy Bohdan, didn't make the final decision to participate in the presidential campaign until December 31, 2018.

It is clear that, for Zelensky and his associates, it was a great opportunity to promote the Servant of the People Party, which had been registered in April 2016 before the upcoming parliamentary campaign.

For Ihor Kolomoisky, who had strained relations with Petro Poroshenko, Zelensky became a bargaining chip for both Ukraine's fifth president and his lifelong opponent Yuliya Tymoshenko.

However, according to political strategist Serhiy Haidai, Zelensky's team perceived the presidential election as a kind of game. As he explained to me:

> I had a conversation with people who talked to the Shefir brothers, his business partners. Even when the campaign was in full swing, they did not believe he would win. They thought it could not happen, that Volodymyr was just playing. But when he won, they were even more confused. They didn't know what to do, because they understood what a responsibility it was and that their old life was over. That

there would be no more Kvartal 95, along with all their production companies ... They found themselves in a completely different reality, in which they would have to be completely different people. And they were at a loss; they tried to consult someone. But it's just about them. Because everything was already different for Zelensky himself. I think Bohdan was already telling him: "Now, don't worry, I know what to do, how to do it, we need to move forward." At that time, nobody liked Bohdan very much, because he was too conspicuous next to the president, and it was obvious that he was the driver of this process.

Anyway, the step taken by Volodymyr Zelensky that New Year's Eve would change not only the leisurely paced life of a celebrity. This step would change the rules of the game in Ukrainian politics.

As it happened, on March 22, 2019, one of the participants in the presidential race, the politician Roman Bezsmertny, tried to stop Zelensky and publicly urged him to withdraw from the race. "Remove your documents from the TsBK [Central Election Commission] because it would be an embarrassment and humiliation for the nation," he said.

However, this call remained unheeded.

The result?

Petro Poroshenko would receive a loud slap in the face from voters.

Yuliya Tymoshenko would not be waiting in the wings for her turn to be president.

Oleh Lyashko would get a strong competitor on the political scene and, a few months later, his Radical Party would lose the parliamentary elections.

Colonel Anatoliy Hrytsenko would retire from politics.

Ukraine would get what it wanted – Volodymyr Zelensky.

Episode 3

"Let It Be the Stadium Then!"

On April 19, 2019, the atmosphere in the largest stadium in Ukraine – NSK (National Sports Complex) Olympic Stadium – was frenetic.

Twenty thousand spectators were waiting for the debate between Petro Poroshenko and Volodymyr Zelensky. For the first time in the history of Ukraine's presidential race, the candidates tried to drive each other into a tight corner – accompanied by a roar from the stands. This show was being filmed and broadcast by 150 TV channels.

Throughout almost the entire presidential campaign, Poroshenko's team had allowed themselves to disparage Volodymyr Zelensky. "Hologram," "clown," "Kolomoisky's puppet," "the hand of the Kremlin" – this is a far from complete list of the verbal insults that were repeated by Poroshenko almost every day. He and his political strategists were convinced that candidate Zelensky was an utter waste of time.

According to Poroshenko's team, there would be enough public debate to prove this. Indeed, this would be one of those political all-around competitions in which the then president seemed already to have the upper hand. And Zelensky? What could be expected from a comedian? Memorized speeches? Prompts from advisors? "Yes, I'll run rings round him," Poroshenko must have thought. But he was very wrong about that. As it turned out, Zelensky had been preparing for the debate for a whole week. At least, that's what Andriy Bohdan claims.

It must be said that Poroshenko's team insisted on this debate between the presidential candidates even before the first round of elections. It was already clear by then that there were three main contenders for the presidency – Petro Poroshenko, Volodymyr Zelensky, and Yuliya Tymoshenko. However, the artistic director of Kvartal 95 blatantly ignored the invitation to take part in the debate. But in the period between the first and second rounds of the election, the desire to bring his opponent in from the virtual to the real world and prove his impotency as a politician had already become an obsession among Poroshenko and his staff.

So it was that, after two weeks of discussions, Zelensky invited Poroshenko to a debate, which was set to take place two days before the second round of elections – on April 19 at 7:00 p.m. at the Olympic Stadium. With spectators and TV broadcasts throughout the country – this was Zelensky's condition. Zelensky's video address to Poroshenko was filmed in a cinematic way. He walks along the corridor of the stadium, enters the field in section seventy-three of the stands, and, like a real boxer, invites his opponent to debate.

Obviously, the actor chose his native element – the stage, the audience, applause, spotlights, and TV cameras. After brief negotiations, Poroshenko was forced to agree to this format. His desire to demonstrate the insignificance of his opponent was so great that he agreed to all his terms.

There were two support teams at the stadium. Two stages. Two concerts taking place at the same time. Different sections for Poroshenko's and for Zelensky's supporters. The hosts were popular Ukrainian journalists Olena Frolyak and Andriy Kulykov. Teams of presidential candidates. The only things missing were a display of championship belts of the presidential candidates and introductions such as there are at a boxing match: "Ladies and gentlemen . . ."

People were expecting a show. And they got it.

Poroshenko left his stage and went to the stage set by Zelensky's team. Poroshenko and Zelensky shook hands, and the debate began.

Zelensky was not as helpless as Poroshenko had imagined. What happened on April 19 on the stage of the NSK Olympic Stadium can hardly be called a debate. It was a typical *KVK* (Club of the Cheerful and Quick-Witted) skit.[1] To be more precise, a competition between two captains, in which Zelensky felt like a fish in water. Yes, he had done his homework and made good use of it in his speech. Yes, he called the breakaway DPR militants "insurgents." Yes, he childishly promised that his opponent would face difficult times after the presidential race. But Zelensky looked sincere. This sincerity might have been a bit undermined by his friend and Kvartal colleague Yevhen Koshovy, who appeared on stage wearing a hoody with the inscription "ПОХУЙ" ["I don't give a fuck"].

Discussions between Poroshenko and Zelensky about the future of the country did not go well. This verbal duel is best described as consisting of mutual accusations, public reproaches, political taunts. The comedian accused the fifth president of having corrupt friends, of making blood money, of failing to investigate insurgents involved in the Revolution of Dignity at the Maidan or to take control

---

[1] *KVK* is the acronym for the Ukrainian iteration of the *KVN* Moscow-based comedy game show, and is called *Klub veselykh i kmytlyvykh* in Ukrainian.

in the endless war in the Donbas. In response, Poroshenko rebuked Zelensky for evading conscription, for his lack of political independence and his ties with Kolomoisky, and for his apparent backing by former members of the Party of Regions.

However, Zelensky's stance still defeated Poroshenko, forcing him to kneel at the Olympic Stadium before the families of those who had perished.

"I am not your opponent, I am your verdict." Zelensky's theatrical and emotional phrase, addressed to Poroshenko, seems to have put an end to the debate at the stadium. To be more precise, it terminated Poroshenko's five-year term and launched Zelensky's political career.

With almost the very same mistakes as those of his opponent.

With accusations of corruption against his team.

With his friends and cronies in power.

One thing is absolutely clear: Zelensky could hardly have imagined what challenges awaited him and the country at the end of February 2022. Neither could the country have imagined that, with the start of full-scale war, it would see a completely different president.

Episode 4

Zelensky and Forty-Two Million Presidents

On April 30, 2019, the Central Election Commission announced the final results of the presidential election: 73.22 percent for Volodymyr Zelensky versus 24.45 percent for Petro Poroshenko.

Zelensky's convincing victory left no doubt that he would be at the helm within a few weeks. However, it turned out not to be so easy, as Parliament, in recess in May, could not decide on the date of President Zelensky's inauguration for two weeks. There were public reproaches from Zelensky's team addressed to their opponents, telling them to get their stuff out of Bankova Street and free up their offices. It seemed that the winners were about to lose patience and make the losing party move out of the presidential headquarters without the conventional niceties.

Zelensky understood perfectly well: he, to put it mildly, was not particularly welcome in Ukrainian politics. Even a landslide victory in the election did not make him equal among those who had spent more than a decade in government on the Pechersk Hills in the capital. Zelensky was well aware of this. Therefore, he immediately issued an ultimatum to the Verkhovna Rada (the Parliament of Ukraine): "The inauguration must take place on May 19." Rumor has it that Zelensky insisted on this date following the advice of astrologers. Supposedly, it was a favorable day to start new affairs.

However, Parliament refused Zelensky's request. On Sunday, May 19, the victims of political repression were commemorated, so the people's deputies (members of Parliament) decided to swear the newly elected president into office the next day, May 20. Zelensky did not hide his irritation.

On inauguration day, Constitution Square in front of the Parliament building resembled the sidewalk of the Cannes Film Festival – TV cameras were everywhere, thousands of fans waiting for the star to appear. Zelensky's relatives, friends, and supporters were lined up all the way to the observation deck near the Mariinsky Palace.

Five minutes before 10:00 a.m., Volodymyr Zelensky, accompanied by four security guards, marched to the Rada to the public's applause. The newly elected president was in a good mood, radiating happiness, extending his hand to those who sought to congratulate him. Seeing his friend from Kvartal 95 Studio, Yevhen Koshovy, in the crowd, Zelensky jumped up and kissed his shaved head. And this was probably his last prank as a man free from the presidency.

At 10:01 a.m., Zelensky entered the Verkhovna Rada. In twenty-five minutes, he was sworn in, and he took to the floor in his new capacity.

The sixth president began his speech: "My dear Ukrainians! After winning the election, my 6-year-old son said: 'Dad, I've seen on TV that they say Zelensky is president. It turns out that I'm also president.' At that moment it sounded like a child's joke. But then I realized that it was really true. Because each of us is president."

Standing behind the rostrum of the Verkhovna Rada, whose members were for the most part skeptical of the newly elected man, Zelensky appeared to be enjoying this rejection. I'm sure, if he had been on the stage of Kvartal 95 at that moment, he would have jumped up with his fist raised and exclaimed: "I've beaten you all!" But protocol and the presence of foreign guests forced Zelensky to mind his behavior. But not his words.

In his inaugural speech, President Zelensky had many fine and considerate words to say both to those who were leaving the country and to those who were losing faith in Ukraine in annexed Crimea and the occupied Donbas. He stated that the Ukrainian state needed peace and the country needed a reboot. He looked like someone who had decided to break the system, which would, of course, resist.

It took two months to approve laws on the abolition of parliamentary immunity, illegal self-enrichment, and to vote for a new electoral code, after which there were early parliamentary elections in Ukraine. Zelensky spoke the language of ultimatums. Noise, applause, and disgruntled shouts in the parliamentary hall forced him to utter every word of his speech clearly, with theatrical pauses. At that moment, everything happening under the dome of the Verkhovna Rada resembled the shooting of the next episode of the *Servant of the People* TV series. Zelensky, who demanded the immediate resignation of the head of the SBU, the defense minister, the prosecutor general, and members of the government, lacked only the two machine guns with which his film hero shot the deputies.

The political "dinosaurs" in the hall of the Rada watched Zelensky with scorn and skepticism, as if challenging him to "digest" them. The four ex-presidents sitting in the guest box – Leonid Kravchuk, Leonid Kuchma, Viktor Yushchenko, and Petro Poroshenko – seemed to be thinking something similar. Nobody knew what Viktor Yanukovych (exiled former president) was thinking about in the suburbs of Moscow at that time. But the anxious face of Olena Zelensky, who sat alongside the former presidents, was very eloquent. The first lady was tense and worried. She was one of the few who did not want Zelensky to be president.

At the end of the inauguration, the parliamentary speaker, Andriy Parubiy, smiled and said: "Thank you all for participating in this solemn meeting. It was fun."

Zelensky didn't seem to like this. However, he didn't argue with Parubiy. Leaving the Parliament hall, the president exchanged courtesies with Oleh Lyashko, a man whom he had repeatedly parodied on the stage of Zelensky's *Evening Kvartal* TV show.

"Volodymyr, you started badly, you will end badly!" the leader of the Radical Party exclaimed. In response, Zelensky pointed his index finger at Lyashko.

Zelensky's presidential beginning was cinematically bright, with a well-written script and a well-worked mise-en-scène.

People outside the Rada and in front of their TVs went crazy. Their idol began to tear up the old system like a rag.

A new era had begun – the era of President Zelensky.

Episode 5

Devirtualization of
Servant of the People

In the beginning was the word. Or rather, several words. And, more precisely, the name of the TV series: *Servant of the People*.

Then there was a political party with the same name.

Without an ideology.

Without local party associations.

Without party members.

What's more, it became Servant of the People only because of the renaming of the Party of Decisive Changes.

A kind of virtual political feast in the era of virtual sex and love. With dubious electoral prospects, and whose chairman, Ivan Bakanov, was a lawyer and a childhood friend of Zelensky.

With absolutely nothing behind it, the party already had a 4 percent following in December 2017. Political scientists later gave it 5 percent support, and then 8.7 percent.

Those whose business it was to sell political illusions and the image of Vasyl Holoborodko, the hero of the TV series, felt at ease in the virtual world. In fact, it was Zelensky's reliance on the Servant of the People Party that helped him in his run for president. Despite his being listed as non-partisan and self-nominated on the ballot, everyone understood perfectly well: when you say Servant of the People, you have in mind Zelensky; when you say Zelensky, you have in mind Servant of the People.

After Zelensky's victory in the presidential election, no one had any doubts that the party of which he was the informal leader would become the country's main party.

At the end of May 2019, Ivan Bakanov, who had been interim head of the SBU, was replaced by Dmytro Razumkov, who also became the new leader of the Servant of the People Party. Two weeks later, at a congress at the Kyiv Botanical Garden, the party announced its first hundred candidates, who were going to run in early parliamentary elections.

Zelensky's associates immediately stated that the Servant of the People Party professed the ideology of libertarianism, which is based on the principle of freedom. Later, the president's allies repeatedly tried to amend the party's ideological principles. Ultimately, they said that the Servant of the People professed the ideology of "Ukrainian centrism." However, it is certainly the case that 45 percent of Ukrainians who were willing to vote for them had absolutely no idea about the ideological foundations of their favorite party. For them, Servant of the People just stood for a popular TV series in which Zelensky, in the guise of Vasyl Holoborodko, skillfully defeated the government that hated the people.

For most of its supporters, the Servant of the People Party was political entertainment: a convention with Coca-Cola, pizza, and shawarma (a gyro sandwich), a selfie with a popular actor, memes such as "Let It Be the Stadium Then" and "Let's Beat Them All Together," Zelensky's phenomenal victory, a cinematic inauguration. A young, handsome, and quick-witted leader. It was all part of a big and exciting game. Some would say that the world was changing, and so were the parties. Clearly they weren't modeled of the CPSU (Communist Party of the Soviet Union) with all its tedious meetings, were they? And of course, there is some truth to this.

However, the phenomenon of the Servant of the People Party was precisely the fact that it was perceived as a project of the protagonist of the film version, Vasyl Holoborodko, rather than that of the real president, Volodymyr Zelensky. A real miracle was expected from the party.

During the presidential campaign, Zelensky was repeatedly criticized for the absence of a team. A bunch of people roaming the TV talk shows gave no clue about who the new head of state was going to work with to change the country.

On June 9, at the Servant of the People Party convention, the team finally materialized. There were many unknown names in the first hundred on the party's list. At the convention, it was explained that this was the result of project "Elevator" (that is, a social elevator).

In the top ten of the list were those who had helped Zelensky to victory in the presidential election – the party leader Dmytro Razumkov, Chief of Staff Oleksandr Korniyenko, the presidential representative in the Verkhovna Rada Ruslan Stefanchuk, the CEO of TV channel 1+1 Oleksandr Tkachenko, the lawyer Iryna Venedyktova, and Mykhailo Fedorov, appointed minister of digital transformation – none of which, in fact, surprised anyone.

During that month, Dmytro Razumkov promised to elaborate on the party's list of candidates and those who would run in the majority constituencies under the Servant of the People banner. According to him, if, God forbid, someone were to cast a shadow on the impeccable reputation of the project, he or she would have to leave the team. Almost no one had any doubt that this would actually happen. The party was new. Personnel errors were possible. No one was insured against them. The only question was whether the price of these mistakes would eventually be too high for the country and, in addition, for their leader, Volodymyr Zelensky.

Everything that took place in May–June 2019 in the new president's team resembled a trip on an ocean liner. Passengers were boarding the ship called *Power*; cheerful music was being played; everyone was looking forward to the holiday. And no one even suspected that this liner could prove to be another political *Titanic*. As has happened many times in Ukrainian politics. Leonid Kuchma, Viktor Yushchenko, Viktor Yanukovych, and Petro Poroshenko all had their own presidential parties, all of which sank into oblivion. Did Zelensky know this? Certainly. Ever since he became president, we have been watching the Servant of the People Party become a political *Titanic*; only the Russian invasion in 2022 prevented it from sinking to the bottom.

It has to be said that Ukrainians are accustomed to believing in myths: in the gold of Hetman Polubotok,[1] which is allegedly kept somewhere in Britain, in the messianism of Viktor Yushchenko, in the fact that all their problems would be solved by Zelensky and his party. Just like in the movies. But people have completely forgotten that the Servant of the People Party is not a TV series about Holoborodko and his bicycle. It represents themselves and the future of their children. They trusted Zelensky and his team. Whether or not this decision was correct will become clear in the aftermath of the Russo-Ukrainian war, because it has been up to Zelensky and the Servant of the People not only to fulfill their election promises, but literally to fight for Ukrainian independence.

---

[1] For information on the legend of Polubotok's gold, see https://en.wikipedia.org/wiki/Gold_of_Polubotok.

Episode 6

A Mad Printer for the President

After the decision had been taken to dissolve Parliament, Zelensky depended on high expectations for early elections to the Verkhovna Rada, scheduled for July 21, 2019. The president and his team hoped to get at least a third of the seats, if not the majority, of the highest legislative body.

In the end, the election results exceeded all expectations of the Zelensky team – 43.16 percent voted for the Servant of the People Party. Another 130 of their candidates won in the majority constituencies. As a result, the "servants" won 254 seats in the Rada. For the first time in the history of independent Ukraine, one party held a majority in Parliament.

On the political sidelines, there were jokes about the fact that all 254 deputies entered the Rada on a single passport – President Zelensky's – and this observation is very appropriate. Because, thanks to Zelensky, the unemployed, wedding photographers, showmen, and restaurateurs, most with very average educational backgrounds and limited knowledge, won parliamentary seats. People who, without

Volodymyr Zelensky, would never have found themselves involved in Ukrainian politics.

The president did not conceal his pride in his political success. The Verkhovna Rada, which started work on August 29, took only twelve hours to completely transform the country's leadership, from ministers to the prosecutor general. No consultations, no negotiations with representatives of other political forces, no protests.

There were no upheavals among Zelensky's personnel. His childhood friend and former head of Kvartal 95, Ivan Bakanov, headed the SBU. Oleksiy Honcharuk, who had been deputy head of the Office of the President for the previous three months, became prime minister. Another deputy head of the presidential office, Ruslan Ryaboshapka, became prosecutor general, and Vadym Prystaiko became minister of foreign affairs.

The average age of those appointed to the government on August 29 was between 30 and 40. They were all new faces in Ukrainian politics, except for interior minister Arsen Avakov, who had survived three cabinets and two presidents.

Following a simplified procedure, Zelensky's associates, at lightning speed, passed dozens of bills over the course of just a few days. The "servants" themselves referred to their way of working as being like a "mad printer" that was shooting out copies of the new laws. However, other participants in the country's political process thought of it as the work of an asphalt paver. With no room to maneuver. With the driver operating one hell of a machine. With everything going under the asphalt – without any discussion. The asphalt layer is the only one working. Everyone else is resting.

Even during the presidential campaign, Zelensky's opponents spoke about the need for Ukraine's transition to a parliamentary republic, which would supposedly reduce the role of the head of state to ritual functions. No more. Indeed, after the tremendous success of the Servant of the People in the Rada elections, this topic became utterly irrelevant.

De facto, starting from August 29, 2019, all power in Ukraine passed solely into the hands of Volodymyr Zelensky. The Verkhovna Rada became one of the divisions of the Office of the President. The "mad printer" was operated by two of Zelensky's associates – the parliamentary speaker Dmytro Razumkov and his first deputy Ruslan Stefanchuk, former star of the Khmelnytsky *KVK* Three Fat Men team. The control of parliamentary committees by the "servants," the observance of the rules of procedure, and the way in which bills were introduced in Parliament reduced other members of the Rada to mere extras.

Nothing, it seemed, could prevent Zelensky and his team from carrying out rapid and necessary reforms for Ukraine.

But after a while, the lack of competition in Parliament, the monopolistic position of one political party, the adoption of important decisions outside the walls of Parliament, and their further legalization by deputies all served to deflate the role of the highest legislative body in the Ukrainian government.

The deputies from the Servant of the People Party would become objects of public ridicule.

Maksym Buzhansky would publicly call one journalist a "stupid sheep."

In a letter, Mykhailo Radutsky would call the head of the ministry of health, Zoriana Skaletska, "our person" and suggest that other candidates "go f... themselves."

Bohdan Yaremenko would be pictured using a dating app while sitting in Parliament.

Serhiy Brahar would suggest that a pensioner should sell her dog to pay for her utilities.

Halyna Tretyakova would divide Ukrainian children into high- and low-quality categories.

Davyd Arakhamiya and Oleksandr Korniyenko would call their fellow female party members "fuglies" and "lanky legsters."

Mykola Tyshchenko's Velyur Restaurant, right in the center of Kyiv, would stay open during the Covid-19 lockdown.

Oleksandr Dubynsky would tell stories about his mother loving to drive fast, thereby explaining the seventeen cars listed in his personal property declaration.

Ruslan Stefanchuk would receive accommodation expenses of 20,000 hryvnias (about $700) per month while living in his mother-in-law's apartment.

Yuriy Koryavchenkov (the actor "Yuzyk" in the Kvartal 95 comedy troupe) would bring the Kryvyi Rih police to heel and explain how Oleksandra Klitina slept her way to the job of deputy minister of infrastructure.

Alexander Trukhin, under the influence of alcohol, would cause an accident on the highway.

Eleven "servant" deputies would be suspected of receiving bribes of $30,000.

And the Servant of the People's deputy Oleksandr Yurchenko would be accused of intending to receive $300,000 for the introduction of certain proposals in one of the bills.

This would all happen later. It's what happens when the hype becomes an integral part of the information policy of the presidential party.

Episode 7

Trump's Impeachment

Zelensky the actor has always dreamt of Hollywood. Sure enough, of the Oscars as well.

Do you recall how Zelensky stared into Tom Cruise's eyes when he arrived in Kyiv and how he couldn't let go of the American actor's hand in his office on Bankova Street?

But he is unlikely to have gone very far in his dreams. For example, he could hardly have imagined himself as a participant in the scandal that was about to result in the impeachment of the 45th president of the United States.

On July 25, 2019, Zelensky received a call from Donald Trump.

This was not their first conversation. On April 21, the day of Zelensky's election victory, he had been personally congratulated by Trump. However, on this occasion the US president asked him to take a closer look at the case of Joe Biden, or rather that of his son Hunter: "There's a lot of talk about Biden's son, that Biden stopped the prosecution, and a lot of people want to find out about that, so whatever you can do with the attorney-general would be great . . . Biden went around bragging that he stopped the prosecution, so if you can look into it . . . It sounds horrible to me," Trump complained to Zelensky.

In response, Zelensky promised to look into the case, hinting that he would soon have a prosecutor general who would be 100 percent his person, and added: "With regard to the US ambassador to Ukraine, as far as I can remember, her name is Yovanovitch [Marie Yovanovitch, US Ambassador to Ukraine 2016–19]. It was great that you were the first to tell me that she was a bad ambassador, because I agree with you 100 percent. Her attitude toward me was far from good, as she admired the previous president and was on his side. She would not readily accept me as the new president."

Ruslan Ryaboshapka became President Zelensky's first prosecutor general. However, he says he never felt fully established. Ryaboshapka remembered it as follows:

I did not have that feeling at all. Honestly, I didn't even think about it. There was some anxiety, because I realized that the work was extremely complicated, difficult, with an extraordinary number of challenges and risks. Truth be told, I was thinking about something else, not about this conversation between Zelensky and Trump. I was speaking of the challenges and risks that I faced in this position. It is common knowledge that I have repeatedly offered to resign from this post, despite the fact that it is one of the highest in the country. I understood that taking over this position is a huge sacrifice and that during my entire term in office I would have no private life at all.

It was kind of the reverse. Zelensky did not tell me what he expected from me; rather, I explained to him how I could be useful in this position. Our top priority didn't have to be charges and criminal cases against Poroshenko or anyone else, but, instead, the reform of the institution of the prosecutor's office. We talked about it. And I saw that as my main task.

Neither Trump nor Zelensky expected the content of their conversation to trigger a huge scandal in the United States.

On September 20, *The Washington Post* reported, citing its own sources, that a US intelligence official had filed a formal complaint over the content of Trump's telephone conversation with a foreign leader, whose name they chose not to mention. The US Congress responded immediately by initiating a formal investigation into the White House incumbent and by demanding the release of a full transcript of the conversation. Volodymyr Zelensky was the foreign leader.

The American press urged Trump to put pressure on his Ukrainian counterpart to speed up the investigation into Biden's son, who was a member of the board of directors of the Burisma Ukrainian gas company. The owner of this company was Mykola Zlochevsky, minister of ecology and natural resources during Viktor Yanukovych's presidency.

Ukraine's Office of the Prosecutor General (HPU) accused the ex-minister of illegal self-enrichment. However, shortly afterward, all Burisma cases were closed, the company repaid tax debts, Attorney-General Viktor Shokin was fired (as a result of the Burisma investigation, according to Trump's lawyer Rudy Giuliani) – but stories concerning the younger Biden continued to circulate.

As the scandal escalated, Zelensky, whose name did not appear on the front pages of the American press, insisted that Trump did not put pressure on him. Given that he was the leader of an independent state, who would dare to try to influence him?

However, in the United States this opinion wasn't shared. And in December 2019, Trump became the third president in US history to be impeached. He was accused of abuse of power and obstruction of justice, based on his telephone conversation with Zelensky. However, on February 5, 2020, the Senate acquitted Trump on both charges.

The story of Joe Biden's son was very similar to that of Paul Manafort, when Ukraine also remained on the front pages of the US press. In 2016, when the US presidential campaign was in full swing, excerpts from the so-called "black book-keeping" of the Party of Regions were published in Kyiv. The then head of Trump's election campaign was mentioned as being among the recipients of cash from Viktor Yanukovych's allies. As a result, Manafort resigned and was later sentenced to seven and a half years in prison on other charges in the United States. Trump viewed publication of the excerpts as Kyiv's way of getting back at him, and Petro Poroshenko had an uphill struggle trying to restore relations with the White House.

The impeachment of Trump would make a great plot for a Hollywood movie in which the role of President Zelensky could easily be played by the actor Zelensky. However, ironically, Joe Biden, against whom Trump was gnashing his teeth, became one of those people who actively supported both Zelensky and Ukraine following the large-scale Russian aggression in 2022. And if Zelensky had accepted Trump's proposal in summer 2019 and reopened the case against the younger Biden, who knows how the relationship between the senior Biden and Zelensky would have turned out. It is hard to say whether Ukraine would have received US assistance in its confrontation with Russia.

Episode 8

Vice-President Bohdan

A joker, a hedonist, a sybarite, a political prankster, and a violator of all written and unwritten rules, Andriy Bohdan has been, and always will be, a colorful character in Volodymyr Zelensky's circle. Hardly anyone can surpass him in terms of arrogance, as can be demonstrated by the fact that the world revolves around him and not the other way around.

Legends have arisen about this lover of vacations abroad on his yacht and the owner of a Tesla, about how he knocked out the tooth of the head of the SBU Ivan Bakanov and ignored the rules set by Zelensky, about his seemingly sudden resignation in July 2019 and how he fought for access to the state's president.

Bohdan himself is proud to have persuaded Zelensky to run for president. While still an advisor to Ihor Kolomoisky, who was head of the Dnipropetrovsk ODA (Regional State Administration), Bohdan suggested that the artistic director of Kvartal 95 Studio run in the special election in the precinct in which Borys Filatov (who left the post to become a mayor) had won back in 2015. However, at that point Zelensky refused.

At that time, Bohdan, who graduated from the Law School of Lviv State University (where his father, Yosyp Hnatovych, was an associate professor in the department of civil law and procedure), had already worked for the Western Railroad under the famous Heorhiy Kirpa. When the latter was appointed minister of transportation, Bohdan moved to Kyiv. He was a lawyer, deputy minister of justice, an advisor to the people's deputy of Ukraine Andriy Portnov, on a voluntary basis, and a government commissioner for anti-corruption policy. Bohdan ran twice for the Verkhovna Rada – in 2007 for the Our Ukraine: The People's Self-Defense Party and in 2014 from the BPP (Petro Poroshenko Bloc). However, he never made it to Parliament. In the first case, his position on the party list was not high enough to make it through. In the second, "Bohdan's law," passed in February 2016, became an obstacle. It allowed party leaders to exclude candidates from the voter lists after the election.

According to Serhiy Leshchenko, a former people's deputy from the BPP, the law was passed specifically to prevent Bohdan, then a lawyer for businessman Hennadiy Korban, from joining the Verkhovna Rada.

As Bohdan himself remembers it, in 2017, while visiting the Vatican, he wrote a humorous post on social media: "I talked to the Pope. He told me that Volodymyr Zelensky would be president." "Of course, it was a joke, but I studied sociology, which taught that society needs new faces," the former head of the Office of the President said to Dmytro Gordon on September 9, 2020.

A year before the presidential election, Bohdan met with Zelensky and encouraged him to run for president. All this time Bohdan worked with Ihor Kolomoisky and his Privat Banking Group. So it needs to be remembered that Bohdan was the link that connected Kolomoisky and Zelensky. Even before his presidency, Bohdan had accompanied Zelensky on his trips to Geneva and Tel Aviv, where the Ukrainian oligarch lived.

But, whatever the case, in 2018 Andriy Bohdan became one of Volodymyr Zelensky's confidants. He was much more knowledgeable about Ukrainian politics than the presidential candidate himself. The personal lawyer of the oligarch Ihor Kolomoisky and the businessman Hennadiy Korban, Bohdan worked in government and had intimate knowledge of all the intrigues, which seemed to be exactly what the political neophyte, the artistic director of Kvartal 95 Studio, needed.

Bohdan seemed to be pursuing a personal agenda in becoming part of Zelensky's team. He wanted to prove to Petro Poroshenko that the latter should not have filed criminal cases against him and should not have removed him from his party list. Nevertheless, he says that he no longer bears a grudge against Poroshenko and speaks with irony about the seat in Parliament that he never took. As it happens, regarding Bohdan's lawsuit in October 2019, the court overturned the decision to exclude him from the BPP list. He has known Poroshenko since 2004, when he worked in the legal department of the Our Ukraine Party during Yushchenko's presidential campaign.

It should be noted that during the 2019 presidential campaign, Bohdan, like Zelensky, avoided excessive publicity. He appeared on TV several times, but that was all. Still, it was Bohdan who stood next to Zelensky whispering something in his ear during the debate with Poroshenko at the Olympic Stadium. It is this image of Bohdan constantly prompting Zelensky that will remain with people for a long time. He would, after all, perceive Zelensky's victory in the election as his own.

I observed something similar in July 1994 after Leonid Kuchma's victory. At that time, Dmytro Tabachnyk, who would later become head of the Office of the President, was as proud as a peacock. Tabachnyk, like Bohdan, did not behave himself – he would interrupt the president in conversation with others, whisper into Kuchma's ear, or simply demonstrate that he was, if not the first person in the state, then at least the second. Pride and arrogance led Tabachnyk to resign as head of the Office of the President. Bohdan walked the same path.

In the early months of his presidency, Zelensky could not manage without Bohdan. To keep him close by, Zelensky even changed the name of the administration to the Office of the President (because otherwise, Bohdan, under lustration because of his work for Yanukovych's team, could not run the presidential office). Bohdan was Zelensky's constant companion wherever he went – on business as well as private trips. He was with him at factories, sports events, and concerts. Everywhere.

He took selfies with the Zelenskys at Niagara Falls and, separately, of himself in swimming trunks, with Zelensky on the Langeron beach in Odesa. He provided the president with answers to the most difficult questions and advised him on personnel decisions. It seemed that Bohdan's strength and omnipotence could be surpassed by no one. This opinion was shared by the head of the Office of the President himself, who, when in public, granted himself more and more power than was appropriate. In summer 2019, the Office of the President allowed information about the resignation statement, allegedly written by Andriy Bohdan himself, to be "leaked" to the media. Hundreds of media outlets, citing their own sources, wrote about it. And then it turned out that, by doing this, the Office of the President had pulled the wool over the eyes of journalists, whom Bohdan himself called nothing but "zhurna . . . liukhy," a blend of "journalists and whores." Moreover, Bohdan overtly stated that the president did not need journalists to communicate with the public.

Then there were conflicts between the head of the Office of the President and the mayor of Kyiv Vitaliy Klitschko, telephone conversations with the then director of the DBR (State Bureau of Investigation) Roman Truba, which were later leaked to the Internet, posts along the line of "Boredom" on his Facebook page, and many other of Bohdan's antics that no one could explain.

Already in autumn 2019, rumors of reducing Bohdan's influence and strengthening the position of another Andriy – Yermak – in Zelensky's coterie were circulating on the political sidelines. The head of the Office of the President obviously understood perfectly well that he was being pushed out of Bankova Street. But he still hoped this would not happen. In December 2019, Zelensky offered Bohdan the position of prosecutor general. But he refused it. "At that time, our internal misunderstandings reached a climax and he made it clear that he did not mind if I took a different job," Bohdan recalls.

However, in January 2020 it became clear that Yermak was shoring up his position with the president. Because it was he, not Bohdan, who flew with Zelensky to Oman. Afterward, he was in charge of negotiations with Iran following the downing of the Ukrainian Boeing passenger jet. And Yermak, not Bohdan, was negotiating with Moscow.

On February 11, 2020, President Zelensky officially fired Andriy Bohdan. The day before, the two had put an end to their relationship, deciding to go their separate ways in politics. Zelensky told Bohdan that he treated him like an unloved wife. He said, as the former head of the Office of the President later reported it: "I don't know what you're doing right, what you're doing wrong, but you're making me angry no matter what you do."

Four months later, Zelensky would say that Bohdan, being the de facto vice-president, showed power where it was not needed, and generally created conflict among the team. In response, Bohdan wrote on Facebook:

> Dear Volodymyr Oleksandrovych, I wanted to respond to your interview.
>
> The rules of business ethics do not allow decent people to comment on their joint activities, even if these people have split up. Of course, this rule is often violated in Ukraine, and I, as a lawyer, including yours, can tell and have told you hundreds of stories about how it ends (which never does any good).
>
> Of course, I am a bearer of knowledge that is very sensitive for you and for the country, but believe me, I will always be a decent person.
>
> As for depriving me of power, I am so grateful to you, because my name will not be related to the chaos into which you are throwing the country. Let me remind you of one of my agreements with you – I promised to work honestly with you until you let me go. Because I was not a gold digger, but rather a dreamer who wanted to see his dream come true. And I have done a lot in six months – you and my team concentrated absolute power in the country in a democratic way, which you have turned into a laughingstock in four months.
>
> I sincerely regret that you have exchanged our dreams of a country of happy people, where there is no corruption, for a warm bathtub for yourself and the cheap whims of the unprofessional and narcissistic people manipulating you.
>
> Sincerely,
>
> Andriy Bohdan.

It can be assumed that, in his message, the former head

of the Office of the President made it clear to Zelensky that he'd better not break off with him completely. Because the former mischief-maker is, as he put it, "the bearer of very sensitive knowledge" concerning people surrounding the head of state. What looked like comedy and misunderstanding yesterday could be a tragedy tomorrow.

On August 11, 2020, Andriy Bohdan's favorite Tesla was set alight. At the same time, his driver's Skoda was set on fire in another district of Kyiv, an event that Bohdan himself does not perceive as a coincidence. He mentioned this in a four-and-a-half-hour interview with Dmytro Gordon on September 9. During this conversation, Bohdan talked a lot about himself, about Zelensky, and about the president's current entourage. The result was that the DBR became interested in Bohdan's statement regarding possible ties between senior Ukrainian officials and Moscow.

"I used to consider Zelensky my friend, but now I don't. He has to wake up, he is not a sleeping beauty. It is necessary to put your mind into everything and understand, to be an expert on each question. You can't replace 'good' or 'bad' with 'like' or 'don't like'," Bohdan said to Dmytro Gordon. At the same time, the ex-head of the chancellery talked a lot about Zelensky's rather limited knowledge of the state system.

Roman Bezsmertny, who has known Andriy Bohdan since the days of the Our Ukraine Party, claims that the former head of the Office of the President is not very different from his former boss. Bezsmertny recalls how, in summer 2019, when he represented Ukraine in the tripartite contact group in Minsk, he met with Bohdan. As Bezsmertny convincingly stated:

Yes, I have known him from the Our Ukraine Party, but the street is one thing, and the head of the Office of the

President is quite another; in Ukraine, this person is, in effect, the prime minister. When our conversation ended and when I called his friend to remove Bohdan from the Office of the President, I felt as if I had taken poison, I was shivering, but I knew for sure that I would survive because I am strong and healthy.

And I also thought about Ukraine: what can these people do with Ukraine when they have no idea how the state machine works? And Bohdan should not be offended by his dismissal. Because it was not really Zelensky, but Almighty God who saved him from the prison that was waiting for him. Those letters he wrote to ministers, which everyone has forgotten today, for whom he set tasks, telling them to whom, and which, grants should be given: I don't think Zelensky knew anything about those letters. They will surface someday, but no one will mention the abuse of power.

One thing is clear about the "virtual" verbal discussion, which Zelensky and Bohdan held literally at the last moment: power changed not only Bohdan, but also Zelensky. During his presidency, Zelensky has become accustomed to being head of state and has gained political experience: he became different. But Bohdan remained as he always was. And I must say that, in February 2022, despite all the public mocking of each other, both men defended Ukraine. The first, as the Supreme Commander-in-Chief of the Armed Forces of Ukraine; the second, as a participant in territorial defense. Andriy said that he tried to contact Zelensky, but he did not answer his call. However, if both once used to fight with each other, now they are fighting against a single enemy – Putin.

Episode 9

The Cosmic Year of 1978

On January 25, 1978, a boy named Volodymyr was born into the family of Oleksandr and Rimma Zelensky in Kryvyi Rih.[1]

The city is one of the largest in Ukraine, although it does not have the status of a regional center.

However, it has always considered itself great, influential, and powerful. Stretching for almost 100 kilometers, Kryvyi Rih was one of the most polluted cities in the former USSR. Iron-ore mining and metallurgy constituted the core of its industry. The city of miners and metallurgists lived by unwritten laws, with certain traditions and rules. In the mid-1960s, the city's population already exceeded 500,000, some of whom were migrants from different parts of the country. A large industrial city needed a lot of manpower. And those people, in turn, needed food and entertainment.

The city really was a complex place. In June 1963, it survived the so-called Riot in a Socialist Town.

---

[1] The name of the city means "crooked ravine," "crooked horn," or "crooked cape."

It all started on June 16, when a soldier named Taranenko was drunk and smoking on a tram. Passengers remonstrated with him, but he took no notice. A policeman by the name of Panchenko happened to be on the same tram and managed to bring the hooligan to his senses. The cop was also a bit tipsy and decided to detain the soldier, who tried to escape. Colleagues of the policeman started firing. A young man and a girl were wounded. Taranenko was detained and beaten up.

Then events unfolded just like in a movie: a crowd gathered near the regional department and began to demand that the policeman be punished. It all ended with widescale riots as well as fights and public disobedience against the authorities, who were forced to use troops and tanks to quell the violence, killing seven people and wounding more than two hundred. Forty-one participants in the riot were put on trial and sentenced to ten years in a maximum security prison. It was a showcase trial that took place in the "Communist" House of Culture.

I mention all this for a reason, so that you can understand how complex a place Kryvyi Rih was, and is – the city where the future president of Ukraine, Volodymyr Zelensky, was born and raised, whose war veteran grandfather, by the way, worked for the police during those turbulent years.

At the same time, in 1978, the Soviet Union continued to actively explore space. On January 10, the Soyuz-27 spacecraft, piloted by Vladimir Yanibekov and Oleg Makarov, was launched from the Baikonur Cosmodrome in Kazakhstan, and, on March 2, the Soyuz-28 spacecraft was launched with Aleksei Gubarev and the Czech Vladimir Remek on board. Soyuz-29, Soyuz-30, and Soyuz-31 followed. All this happened in one year. The USSR was trying to demonstrate its superiority in the world arena. The attempt to catch up and overtake capitalism took place against the backdrop of a rather modest Soviet lifestyle, where purchasing a refrigerator, washing machine, or TV in installments was considered seventh heaven, and buying Yugoslavian shoes in a store was like hitting the jackpot. The country spending hundreds of millions on space exploration could scarcely provide heating to rural school bathrooms.

In Ukraine, the KGB was exterminating the Ukrainian Helsinki Group, which was fighting for human rights in the USSR. Mykola Rudenko and Levko Lukyanenko were imprisoned. Myroslav Marynovych, Mykola Matusevych, and Petro Vins were also put behind bars. The role of censorship was growing in the republic. Volodymyr Shcherbytsky, the first secretary of the CPU (Communist Party of Ukraine) Central Committee, fought against dissidents and did his best to please Moscow. The party apparatus underwent russification. It was under Shcherbytsky that the entire ruling elite would switch to speaking Russian, including the leader of the Ukrainian Communists himself, who would use it exclusively at work.

For the future fourth president of Ukraine, Viktor Yanukovych, 1978 would be significant. That year, the then chairman of the Donetsk Regional Court, Vitaliy Boyko, would protest two sentences against Yanukovych for robbery and infliction of moderate bodily harm, dating from 1967 and 1970, and the Presidium of the Donetsk Regional Court would overturn both sentences in the absence of a crime on Yanukovych's part. De facto, 1978 would be the beginning of Yanukovych's career. Later, he became a member of the CPSU and started making his way up the party administrative ladder – all the way to being President of Ukraine. According to one version, Yanukovych's fate was also decided by Soviet space or, more precisely, by the two-time hero of the Soviet Union, the cosmonaut Heorhiy Berehovy. Rumor had it that he was Yanukovych's father. In any case, someone's powerful hand helped Yanukovych clear his criminal record, paving his way to power.

Thirty-two years later, Yanukovych, rehabilitated in 1978, would meet Volodymyr Zelensky, born in 1978. This happened on July 10, 2010. On that day, the southern coast of Crimea was paralyzed, literally. Guests were rushing to the Zorya state *dacha* (summer residence) No. 11 in the town of Foros to attend Yanukovych's sixtieth birthday party. Zelensky, with Kvartal 95, was among the actors entertaining Yanukovych's guests. Late in the evening, Zelensky's tired team returned to the Yalta Hotel, where a delegation of Ukrainian journalists was also staying (the author of this book among them). They had come at the invitation of former Yalta Mayor Serhiy Braik.

Four years later, Yanukovych would flee to Russia.

Nine years later, the man who entertained Viktor Yanukovych and his guests in Foros would become the sixth president of Ukraine. But 1978 remained the starting point for both: Yanukovych took the first steps on his career path; Zelensky took his first steps on earth.

The last time the paths of Zelensky and Yanukovych crossed was in March 2022, when the war between Russia and Ukraine was already in full swing. Yanukovych, whom Putin planned to return to "reign" in Kyiv, addressed Zelensky publicly and advised him to surrender:

> I want to address Volodymyr Zelensky in a presidential and even a slightly paternalistic way . . . I understand very well that you have many "advisors," but you personally are obliged to stop the bloodshed at all costs and reach a peace agreement. This is what is expected of you in Ukraine, the Donbas, and Russia. The Ukrainian people and your partners in the West will be grateful to you for this.

Zelensky ignored this appeal. The absence of response was his most eloquent answer to Yanukovych. As well as the fact that, unlike Yanukovych, he did not abandon Ukraine at a difficult time for the country.

Episode 10

The Irreplaceable Yuliya Mendel

In September 2009, at the Lviv Publishers' Forum, I was approached by a young journalist with a microphone from the ICTV channel. "Serhii, can I talk to you for a moment?" she asked, and introduced herself: "Yuliya Mendel." I don't remember exactly what we talked about then, but it must have been about books.

Six years later, I met Mendel on the Espresso TV channel. I had been appointed editor-in-chief of the site, and she was to do two programs there – *Hello from Europe* and *Without Words*. However, we ended up not working together for very long – after just a few months Mendel's projects were canceled, and she herself said that this was due to her story about corruption in the Ukrzaliznytsia Railway Company.

Since 2015, our paths have not crossed. First she worked as a correspondent for TV Channel 112 and then for Inter TV in the United States. Yuliya Mendel was a freelance writer for the *New York Times* and a communications consultant for the World Bank in Ukraine. It was not until June 2019, after her appointment as a press secretary, that our paths crossed virtually – though not for long. Because,

after a nine-year friendship on Facebook, I received noti-
fication, along with most of her old friends, that she had
unsubscribed.

The Office of the President announced Yuliya Mendel's
name on June 3, 2019. She had won the competition for the
post of press secretary, which was initiated by Zelensky's
team at the end of April and in which more than 4,000
candidates took part. Why the new president chose
Mendel remains a mystery. Mendel herself says that she
met Zelensky during a group interview with the *New York
Times*. And at her final interview for the position of press
secretary, Zelensky tested her English.

At the time of her appointment, Mendel was a 32-year-old
graduate of the Institute of Philology at Taras Shevchenko
National University of Kyiv. She was born in Henichesk,
Kherson Region, to a family of medical doctors. She held
a Candidate of Philological Sciences Degree (similar to a
PhD) and had been an intern at the Euro-Atlantic Academy
in Warsaw and at Yale University. In an interview with
Nataliya Vlashchenko, Mendel said that she was born into
quite a poor family; they were starving in the 1990s. And
that she fought corruption while defending her candidate's
thesis. And that, in 2016, she decided to put an end to her
television journalism and spend her last $3,000 to train at
Yale. However, instead, she ended up in a job in the United
States for the Inter TV channel.

Before joining the Office of the President, Yuliya Mendel
cannot be said to have had any relevant experience. There
are hundreds, if not thousands, of such media people in
Ukraine. And yet it was Mendel who joined the presidential
team, where she began to interpret her main mission in her
own way.

There was demonstrative disregard for former colleagues,
attempts to push them away from Zelensky, geographical

ignorance when she confused Lithuania with Latvia and Ottawa with Toronto, inappropriate comments on the situation in the Donbas, where she alleged Ukrainian military were shelling cities, and many other screwups that would normally have put an end to any presidential spokesperson's career. But not in Mendel's case. And this was because she was given much more slack than her position formally provided. When journalists demanded that the Office of the President fire her for unprofessionalism – for obstructing the work of Radio Liberty journalists Serhiy Andrushko and Christopher Miller – Zelensky publicly defended her: "I have to say to her: 'This is no good. Should you do it again we'll have to say goodbye to you.' But for now I'm defending her . . . To err is human. That's why I will defend her in this case."

Yuliya Mendel considers herself a member of Zelensky's team, a diplomat, a communicator. However, a rather injudicious photo of Mendel together with the head of state during an interview with the *Guardian* in March 2020, where he is sitting and she is standing with her hand on the back of the president's chair, inspired a flood of photoshopped parodies and ironic ridicule. Because everything looked too intimate, family-like. And Mendel showered compliments on her boss. I think Zelensky liked it. However, this gave rise to new rumors: about an affair between Mendel and the president and even about her possible pregnancy. The discussion of this topic was actively fueled by politician Hennadiy Balashov.

Mendel put up with it for a while, and then wrote a short note on her Instagram page, where she urged Ukrainians not to believe in fake news:

Channel 24 published an article with the names of the top fake news creators of the year.

Read, think, and remember:

> You are what you consume. Especially when it comes
> to information.
> Respect others and, most importantly – respect
> yourself.

Ironically, Mendel, who was in charge of the president's communications with the press, was not herself ready to resist informational provocation. And this is obviously the main outcome of her work as press secretary to the head of state.

At the end of April 2021, Mendel resigned, having written a book, *Each of Us is the President*, in which she spoke about her role in modern Ukrainian politics. She continues to work with Zelensky's team.

Episode 11

Look into the Eyes of Putin and . . .

During the first few months of his presidency, Volodymyr Zelensky sought a meeting with Vladimir Putin. The new leader of Ukraine was anxious to fulfill his campaign promise – to end the war in the Donbas. He understood that his campaign rhetoric, which had been reduced to the formula "just stop shooting," had proved unviable. It was necessary to sit down at the negotiating table with Putin.

Zelensky said he wanted to look the master of the Kremlin in the eye and understand him as a person. For this reason, he was ready for anything – for another truce in the Donbas, even if it did not bring peace; for the dispersal of forces on the front line; for another settlement with Moscow. And this was probably Zelensky's strategic mistake because he wanted to see Putin as a person at the negotiating table, not Putin as an aggressor. Zelensky sincerely believed that, if he looked into the eyes of the Russian president, he would at least see some sign of sadness about the 14,000 dead in the Donbas.

The Ukrainian president seemed convinced that his actor's charisma and unique charm would work wonders in Paris, where the Normandy Four summit was scheduled for December 9, 2019, and he would return home with guarantees of an end to the war in eastern Ukraine. At the same time, Zelensky completely forgot that Putin was no worse an actor than he was. Seriously, Putin had played the role of peacemaking president for twenty years, pretending that "they [the Russians] are not there." In Georgia, the Transnistria region, and Syria. The same in Ukraine.

Zelensky tried to play his part with Moscow in negotiations on the Donbas issue. In summer 2019, he tried to strengthen the team in the Trilateral Contact Group (TCG) in Minsk. On July 9, Roman Bezsmertny was returned to the working group on political issues. He had participated in the negotiation process during Poroshenko's presidency. However, a month later, on August 13, he was removed from office. He told me:

> I told Leonid Danylovych Kuchma overtly, about three weeks before the appointment, that I don't see myself on this team and won't be able to work with them. Because at that time I was aware of who these people are: Zelensky, Korniyenko, Razumkov. Ukraine is a very small country. It is very talkative. And I knew most of these people in person or in absentia. I had been with them through thick and thin by then, so I understood perfectly well that people working with them make stupid decisions. And you could tell this from their very first steps.

Bezsmertny recalls his meeting with Zelensky, who, despite Bezsmertny's remarks during the election campaign, thanked him for agreeing to join the TCG in Minsk. Bezsmertny recalls:

> Here's what I didn't like about this meeting. He [Zelensky] averted his eyes. I always look at my interlocutor straight in

the eye. I looked into his eyes, and he kept averting them. And I understood that it was either part of a game or his emotional state. And when I got out of there, I said in my first interview [after meeting Zelensky] that the president wants the best, but I'm not familiar with the material yet. I saw it, I felt it. I asked him how he sees the situation in the east. He replied that by the New Year, i.e. by 2020, we have to resolve the issue with the Donbas. And I already realized that he had no idea what it was. Because the words "solve the issue with the Donbas" sounded like "tackle corruption," "engage in economic reform" – that is, do nothing. Realizing the weaknesses of the TCG, I asked Zelensky to instruct me on how to prepare the relevant documents. And in two weeks I had a project that was agreed on by all participants of the TCG, and reported to the Secretary of the RNBO and to the head of the Office of the President. After meeting with the head of the Office of the President, Andriy Bohdan, I called a close friend of his and said: "Take him away, otherwise he will be put in jail." The conversation sounded ridiculous, comical, silly, but Bohdan's words about Zelensky's ignorance of how state institutions work (during an interview with Dmytro Gordon in September 2020) were more about Bohdan himself.

They simply couldn't figure out what to do or how. I saw confusion, which was in no way different from the confusion of 2013. Only in 2019, the frontline was already set. There were enough combat units already fighting and able to respond automatically. And the system, the institutions of power, the supreme command, and especially the Supreme Commander-in-Chief, did not acknowledge these problems at all. At that moment, I didn't remain silent. In fact, this was the reason for my resignation.

On October 1, 2019, former President Leonid Kuchma agreed on the so-called Steinmeier Formula in the Minsk

TCG. According to the formula, the parties agreed to a ceasefire, the withdrawal of troops, the Verkhovna Rada's adoption of a law on amnesty for militants, and to holding local elections under the auspices of the OSCE (Organization for Security and Cooperation in Europe). This formula was perceived by some Ukrainians as surrender, and in many cities there were "No to capitulation" protests to prevent the implementation of this plan as part of the expected Normandy Four summit in Paris. But the most interesting thing is that, at the end of October, former President Leonid Kuchma himself stated that, in its current form, the Steinmeier formula was unacceptable to Ukraine.

On the eve of the summit, December 8, about 10,000 participants of the Red Lines for Zelensky Chamber gathered on the Maidan (Independence Square) in Kyiv. During the evening, the Capitulation Resistance Movement staged pickets in front of the Office of the President. The organizers of both events explained their actions as being led by a desire to support Zelensky in Paris. According to them, the Maidan would help the Ukrainian president say a resounding "no" to Putin. In fact, these speeches in the center of Kyiv were, of course, a warning to Zelensky himself.

The Office of the President had its own version of why people were gathering on the Maidan – money. The head of the office, Andriy Bohdan, was convinced that this was the work of former President Poroshenko. "Roshenkas" (candy from the ROSHEN factory, which belongs to Poroshenko) were allegedly put into everyone's pockets, and so they bought it. Nevertheless, there were representatives of the political parties Batkivshchyna (Fatherland), Holos (Voice) and Democratychna Sokyra (Democratic Ax) on the Maidan, as well as war veterans and public activists. And the reason for coming to the Office of the President was not money, but the lack of a clearly articulated position by Zelensky on the eve of the Paris summit. All his assurances that he would not surrender sounded unconvincing.

The summit began on December 9 at 4:00 p.m. local time. It was a sunny day. The guard of honor lined up in the courtyard of the Élysée Palace. French President Emmanuel Macron greeted guests on the porch, with journalists standing in front of the guard of honor.

German Chancellor Angela Merkel was the first to arrive. A Mercedes-Benz drove Ms. Merkel almost up to the doorstep of the palace, where, dressed in a blue jacket, she was met and kissed by an elegant and smiling Macron.

A Renault Espace, with Volodymyr Zelensky, was the second car to drive into the courtyard and stop at the gate. The president of Ukraine, wearing a coat, walked briskly toward the president of France. He passed the guard of honor and cheerfully greeted Macron. Against this background, one of the Russian journalists shouted: "Mr. Zelensky, what would be a success for you? Mr. Zelensky! Mr. Zelensky, please answer the question! Mr. Zelensky!" However, Macron and Zelensky ignored the man shouting from the crowd and, like two good friends, marched to the entrance of the palace. Few would remember this, but Macron had been the first foreign leader to meet with Zelensky as a presidential candidate between the first and second rounds of the presidential election. Do you remember that famous photo of Zelensky, Ruslan Ryaboshapka, Oleksandr Danyliuk, and Ivan Bakanov walking around the French capital, and the caption: "Dream team"?

Putin was the last to arrive at the Élysée Palace. He tried not to show any emotion. The master of the Kremlin emerged slowly from the Aurus-41231SB Senat L700 car and just as ponderously plodded around the courtyard, approached Macron, shook his hand, and disappeared inside. This episode was very expressive. The state leader, who was trying to instill fear in Europe and the world, looked old, lame, and was no match for Macron and Zelensky. It was a different era, a different age, a different mentality, a different thirst for life.

There were nine hours of talks ahead as well as Zelensky's debut press conference as a member of the Normandy Four. The very fact that the leaders of Germany, France, Ukraine, and Russia were meeting after a three-year break was already a victory. Behind closed doors, Zelensky met one-on-one with Putin, then with Macron, and later with Merkel. He did not say publicly what he had seen in his Russian counterpart's eyes. Apparently, Putin used his traditional negotiation techniques – blackmail, intimidation, and the carrot-and-stick method.

During the protocol photoshoot before the talks, Zelensky was noticeably nervous. At first, he wanted to take Putin's place, then he turned to talk to journalists and inadvertently showed them some papers. These were his topics for negotiations.

"Once everyone has left," the Russian president told Zelensky, pointing to the person in charge of the photoshoot, "we will start negotiations." The Ukrainian president took a sip of water. His anxiety was obvious.

Then there were the negotiations. And then – the press conference of the Normandy Four and a joint communiqué following the talks, which once again discussed a ceasefire in the Donbas, the exchange of prisoners "all for all," and further deployment of forces in three additional sectors along the line of contact.

Zelensky did not seem impressed by his tête-à-tête with Putin. By the end of the summit, the presidents of Russia and Ukraine had not arrived at a common position on the future of the Donbas, in particular, on the transfer to the Ukrainian side that part of the Russo-Ukrainian border that, legally, belongs to Ukraine but since 2014 has been controlled by the so-called LPR and DPR. Putin was relentless – this was only to be as prescribed in the Minsk agreements, i.e., on the day after the elections in the ORDLO (the temporarily occupied territory of Ukraine). Zelensky was against this and complained about the Minsk agreements, which had been approved by his predecessor Petro Poroshenko. However, in the press release all parties expressed their intention to agree on the legal aspects of the special status of local self-government in the ORDLO and to elaborate on the Steinmeier Formula.

Only a few people know for sure what was really going on behind the scenes at the Paris summit. Interior minister Arsen Avakov praised the Ukrainian president and told reporters that the latter had allegedly asked (Russian foreign minister) Sergei Lavrov not to nod his head. "Volodymyr Zelensky, in conversation, mostly in Russian, finally exploded and said: 'Mr. Lavrov, stop nodding, there is no need to nod! Yes, I know your last name, because, unlike you, I walked around all these places along the border on my own two legs.'"

Later, Putin's aide Vladislav Surkov called the words of the head of the ministry of internal affairs of Ukraine drunken fantasies, since he had apparently finished off all the wine at the end of the summit.

Among those who could tell more, but remained silent, was Andriy Yermak, for whom the meeting of the Normandy Four would be the first, but not the last, serious victory in Volodymyr Zelensky's entourage.

However, the head of the Office of the President, Andriy Bohdan, tried to ignore Yermak's triumph. During Zelensky's conversation with journalists in Paris, Bohdan sang Svyatoslav Vakarchuk's song "Kholodno" ("It's cold") behind Zelensky's back and chanted to the press: "We-tha-a-nk-yo-u-u!"

This seemed to irritate Zelensky. Along with his meeting with Putin, Bohdan's behavior during the summit was no less exasperating.

Two months later, Bohdan resigned as head of the Office of the President. He was replaced by Andriy Yermak, Zelensky's chief negotiator with the Russians, and the next meeting of the Normandy Four, scheduled for March 2020, did not take place, as by then the world was engulfed by the COVID-19 pandemic.

All Zelensky's attempts to negotiate with Putin over the course of two years had failed.

In spring 2021, the Ukrainian president suggested that the master of the Kremlin meet him in the Donbas. Putin replied: "We are interested in the Russian language, the Church, the citizens of the Russian Federation in Ukraine. The Donbas is an internal issue of the Ukrainian state."

Five months later, Russian deputy security secretary Dmitry Medvedev wrote in the Russian *Kommersant* business newspaper that any contact with Ukraine's current leadership was meaningless and Moscow would wait for a change of government in Kyiv.

And four months after that, on February 24, 2022, Putin launched a full-scale invasion of Ukraine.

Despite all this, Zelensky is still ready to meet with the Russian president. However, this would no longer be in order to look him in the eye, but to stop Russian aggression in Ukraine.

Episode 12

The Amateur on an Electric Scooter

Oleksiy Honcharuk was the first and, to date, the last prime minister in the history of modern Ukraine to enter the seat of government on an electric scooter. It happened on Sunday, September 1, 2019, on the eve of the new academic year. The newly appointed head of government decided to start his term in office in a modern way. A polo shirt, jeans, sneakers, and a scooter – all this, obviously, symbolized the end of the era of boring and arrogant "white-collar officials."

Honcharuk rode the scooter through the corridors of the cabinet of ministers, telling schoolchildren: "The Ukrainian government works in this building. Ministers make the most important decisions for the country. But for the country to be successful, we need smart, educated, free citizens. We need you! Therefore, study really well, and we in the government will do everything to create all the necessary conditions for this."

It is unlikely that Honcharuk himself knew then that he would have exactly six months to implement his plan. Honcharuk would leave Zelensky's team at lightning speed, as quickly as he had joined it. Let me remind you that on April 22, 2019, in an interview with the KRYM project, he had praised Petro Poroshenko and been quite skeptical about Volodymyr Zelensky's presidential prospects. As he told the project leader Volodymyr Fedorin:

> We should not forget that under Poroshenko – whether it was good or bad – there was no practice of printing money to fill the gaps. And this was quite an accomplishment . . . And this is exactly what we might lose if the administration of the new president does not understand that the regulator must be independent . . . We do not understand who Zelensky is, so it is incredibly difficult to clarify our attitude toward him . . . If you explain to me who Zelensky is, I'll tell you how I feel about him.

However, a month later, Honcharuk joined Zelensky's team at the invitation of Andriy Bohdan, as deputy head of the office for economic affairs, and would accompany the president on all his trips – both in Ukraine and abroad. And four months later, he was prime minister, becoming, at the age of 35, the government's youngest leader.

Honcharuk studied at the Interregional Academy of Personnel Management (like his predecessor, Volodymyr Groysman) and, at the National Academy of Public Administration, under the president, he worked as a lawyer, advising the environment minister Ihor Shevchenko and the first deputy prime minister Stepan Kubiv; he also ran the Better Regulation Delivery Office – the BRDO. This structure had been created by Aivaras Abromavicius when he was in the government, with financial support from the European Union. Honcharuk and others prepared recommendations for better state regulation in various spheres and, at the same time, implemented the "People are Important" project.

Olena Shulyak, Oleksiy Orzhel, Oleksandr Kubrakov, and Vitaliy Bezhin all joined Parliament from the BRDO, from the list of candidates of the Servant of the People Party. Incidentally, Honcharuk himself also ran for the Rada, but in 2014. He headed the list of candidates of the Power of the People Party, but he lost the election (the party won 0.11 percent of the votes).

After his appointment as prime minister, Honcharuk, elegantly dressed in a pressed three-piece suit, radiated self-confidence. It's true, he had no experience managing businesses. It's also true that he had never headed a ministry before. And, yes, he was in theory an expert. But this, according to the presidential team, was to Honcharuk's advantage, rather than a shortcoming. Zelensky himself has repeatedly spoken in public about the vote of confidence that the young prime minister received from him.

Honcharuk was given the role of showcasing President Zelensky's reforms. But this role quickly bored him. More precisely, he wanted to be a reformer himself, rather than play this role under the sixth president. He was well aware that Zelensky was very weak on economics and public administration, and in general at running the country, but in public he continued to function as the president's loyal armor-bearer.

The country found out what was going on behind the scenes when the content of the prime minister's meeting with finance minister Oksana Markarova, NBU (National Bank of Ukraine) chair Yakiv Smoliy, NBU deputy chair Kateryna Rozhkova, and deputy head of the Office of the President Yuliya Kovaliv, dated December 16, 2019, was leaked to the Internet. A month later, on January 15, 2020, the record itself was made public.

In this conversation, Honcharuk admitted to being an amateur in economics and claimed that Zelensky too only has a very vague idea of economic processes. Or, as Honcharuk put it bluntly, he had "a fog in his head." In short, the prime minister did not speak very highly of the president. But he did it behind the scenes and probably never expected this conversation to be made public.

The question of who and why someone tried to initiate a quarrel between Zelensky and Honcharuk by leaking records to the Internet remains open. Searches of the premises of the TV channel owned by the oligarch Ihor Kolomoisky provided no answers either.

For two days after the recording appeared, Honcharuk repeatedly denied that he would resign.

On the third day, he decided to go, sending his resignation letter not to the Verkhovna Rada, as required by law, but to President Zelensky, probably thinking, it's up to you, father, to decide whether I'm guilty or not.

It seems that this appeal to the president's mercy worked. The head of state and the prime minister met publicly on TV and talked about mutual trust. And that seemed to be the end of the conflict. However, the whole affair did, de facto, put an end to Honcharuk's premiership. Zelensky, apparently, could not put up with what Honcharuk had said: "a fog in his head." Just another month and a half would pass – and then Honcharuk wrote another letter of resignation, approved by the president and Parliament on March 4.

Episode 13
A Little Bell for Maslyakov

Zelensky's career in show business began with *KVK*. The sixth president of Ukraine grew up in the midst of this popular television competitive improvised comedy show, first in the USSR and then in the post-Soviet space.

In 1994, in order to participate in the Premier League of *KVK* in Moscow, two teams – the Zaporizhzhya State Medical Institute and the Kryvyi Rih Hoodlums – created Zaporizhzhya–Kryvyi Rih–Transit, in which Volodymyr Zelensky was invited to take part, first as a dance director, and then as a writer.

It is in this team that the future president of Ukraine would meet the Shefir brothers – Serhiy and Borys, who became his close friends. Together they would conquer Moscow and the show business world and build up their business in Ukraine. After Zelensky's victory in the 2019 presidential election, the brothers became his invaluable supporters.

It was in this team on the Sochi stage in 1997, during the KiViN festival, that Zelensky made his debut as an actor with a short comedy sketch.

It was in this team that Zelensky met Andriy Yakovlev, the future writer for Kvartal 95 Studio and screenwriter of the TV series *The In-laws* and *Servant of the People*; along with the Shefir brothers, he became Zelensky's business partner.

It was in this team that the future president of Ukraine became a champion in the *KVK* Premier League for the only time in his life, even though that victory was shared with the Armenians. But it did happen.

In fact, the 1997 *KVK* final, which took place on December 26, 1997 and brought together two teams, Zaporizhzhya–Kryvyi Rih–Transit and the New Armenians, did not just determine the fate of Zelensky; it was also the impetus for the creation of Kvartal 95. It was a make-or-break game throughout, especially when it came to the final vote for the championship.

It was an epic final. A confrontation. The Zaporizhzhya–Kryvyi Rih–Transit team held the obvious advantage. It ended up in a draw and disappointment. All this happened under the roof of the Moscow Palace of Youth.

The star jury included celebrities Alexander Abdulov, Leonid Parfenov, Konstantin Ernst, Andrei Makarov, Sergei Sholokhov, Sergei Zhigunov, Ivan Demidov, and Yuli Gusman.

Both teams consisted of future show business stars – Garik Martirosian, Artashes Sarkisian, Artur Dzhanibekian, Volodymyr Zelensky, Olena Malyashenko (Kravets), Denys Manzhosov, and Yuriy Krapov.

The Zaporizhzhya–Kryvyi Rih–Transit team, in which Zelensky played, was greeted by fans in the audience with blue and yellow flags and posters: "Even an experienced *dzhigit* [horseman] knows that Transit will win," "Transit is the champion." A year later, in one of his first interviews at the Sochi *KVK* festival, Zelensky shared details of the final:

We understood that the Armenians would win. We wanted to conquer the audience. Every day, on each track, Maslyakov took one musical sketch from us. Actually, we had a brilliant metal screen weighing about 80 kilograms. It was an idiotic locker room. A very interesting sketch for about two minutes. It was discarded. That's how we had three sketches taken from us. Then, in the TV version, they cut out seven jokes that were related to the musical sketch, six jokes from the "Business Card" part of the game, and two segments from the "Homework" sketch. Despite this, we didn't expect such success in the musical part. We were very well received by the audience.

It was already obvious in the musical contest that Transit would become the *KVK* champion. Before the final contest – "Homework" – the New Armenians were losing to the Ukrainian team, although not by much: 15.99 to 16.49. Zelensky's team could already smell victory.

The game ended with an obvious advantage for the Ukrainians. The jury consulted for forty minutes but could not come to an agreement. Then Maslyakov asked that the final contest not be assessed. After that, the director and TV presenter Yuli Gusman made an announcement:

I will tell you what the jury thinks. First, we were all riveted by the performance of the teams. I must say that we did prefer one team throughout most of the game. Another team got to the finals thanks to their youth, humor, and optimism. We got together and looked at the score. We were fearful that a single point might accidentally make a difference, because it is mathematics, a mistake, there are eight of us here, and it might resolve this problem. We don't want that. And so we ask you to support our New Year's decision – to congratulate both teams at this meeting. And we suggest a toast to the health of the winning teams.

Aleksandr Maslyakov, holding the cup, pretended to be utterly confused. "No matter what this or that team wants," Maslyakov pointed to the left and right, "we have to take into account the opinion of the jury. I am going to keep this prize in the club and invite the two teams to stage a rematch next summer. And then we will determine the winner."

The audience accepted this decision with howls. The players of both teams were also dissatisfied.

In summer 1998, the rematch announced by Aleksandr Maslyakov did not take place.

Instead, a new team arrived at the KiViN festival in Sochi – the *KVK* team from Kryvyi Rih, which included former Transit actors Zelensky, Manzhosov, Krapov, and Kravets.

Zelensky himself said then that Kryvyi Rih had its own *KVK* league, in which up to twenty teams played. In an interview for KiViN, he said:

> We decided to skim the cream off these teams – one or two of the best comedians, the best jokes. We ourselves were sitting and writing the sketches. It took about two weeks to prepare. Then we arrived in Sochi. We performed really well at the first preview. I was surprised that we got to the gala concert. Everything was judged fairly. Because we were a poor team. Everyone understands what I'm talking about.

Maslyakov really liked the team and so it got to the gala concert of the festival. Many, many years later, when Zelensky became president, Maslyakov would say that he saw in Volodymyr a talent not only of an actor, but also of an organizer who was able to unite not just the *KVK* community, but also a number of projects.

Incidentally, the part of the president in one of the sketches of the *KVK* team from Kryvyi Rih in Sochi was played by Yuriy Krapov, not by Zelensky. The actor was trying to say something, but no one could understand him. Zelensky then commented on what the audience saw on stage: "You've just watched the New Year's 'turning away'[1] of the president from the people."

At that time, Zelensky is unlikely to have had dreams of becoming president, and even less likely to have imagined any of his future New Year addresses to Ukrainians. In 1998 in Sochi, he wanted one thing – to act in the *KVK* Premier League with a new team, which, after KiViN, became known as Kvartal 95, named after one of the districts in Kryvyi Rih.

A few years would pass, and Volodymyr Zelensky's team became one of the best in Aleksandr Maslyakov's company. Still, Kvartal never succeeded in becoming the *KVK* Premier League champion. Their highest placement was in the semi-finals. Twice the players were awarded second prize at the musical festival "Singing KiViN." Three times the team made it to the final in the Ukrainian league, but not until 2001 was luck on their side. They became the champions. However, wherever they were, just like the Armenians in 1997, the Kvartal performers acted like winners. The frontman of the team played a significant role in that respect.

Zelensky recalls that Kvartal was almost the only Ukrainian team in the *KVK* in the late 1990s. However, it can be considered Ukrainian only in part, since almost all the jokes were focused on Russia. Parodies of Putin and the pop singer Filipp Kirkorov, jokes about the economist Anatoliy Chubais, and about the Russian national soccer

---

[1] A pun is intended here. Instead of the word *obrashchenie* (an address), Zelensky uses the word *otvrashchenie* (a turning away, or revulsion).

team – in short, all this "stuffing" was intended for Russians and those Ukrainians who were under the influence of Russian television.

In 2003, Zelensky and his team decided to leave *KVK*. Kvartal 95 was going to make its own television entertainment shows.

At the end of the year, Zelensky's team, together with the Ukrainian TV channel Studio 1+1 and the Russian TV channel STS, recorded five shows. They were aired in 2004: the anniversary show *Oh! Five 95!*,[1] a concert "The Eighth of Marchie,"[2] a ceremony for the 2004 Golden Pumpkin Award, and a visiting show in Yalta, "Mysterious Island." Maslyakov, of course, took offense at the Kvartal comedians.

Zelensky himself explained the decision to leave Aleksandr Maslyakov in an interview with journalist Dmytro Gordon on the eve of the 2019 presidential election:

> When we were finishing our life as a *KVK* team, I received a fairly simple proposal – to stay on as an editor in the Club of the Cheerful and Quick-Witted but to disband the team. It was a painful decision for me. What does it mean to "disband a group of friends"? What are they, slaves? My answer was "no," I am only with the team. We arrived in Kyiv. We made the first Kvartal show. I started receiving calls. They closed Zhovtnevy Concert Hall. They didn't let me get there first. I'm not even sure whether Maslyakov did it himself. I have no evidence. But we filmed a Kvartal show. And that meant – this is it, you've left the *KVK*. You've become independent and anathematized at the same time. Or so they said. Sometime in 2010 we met Maslyakov. He

---

[1] A pun based on the acoustic similarity to the Russian expression *opiat' dvadtsat' piat* (25 again).

[2] A pun on the name of the month of March meaning something like the eighth of little March.

said: "I know that you are highly respected in Ukraine. I am
happy for your success."

Anyway, one thing is clear, if it weren't for the 1997 *KVK*
final, in which the Zaporizhzhya–Kryvyi Rih–Transit team
ended up in a draw with the New Armenians, the Kvartal
95 team might easily not have emerged. If the Ukrainians
had been the only champions of the Club of the Cheerful
and Quick-Witted, it is possible that the fate of the actors
would have been completely different. Hence the sense of
unfinished business after the 1997 final resulted in Transit,
led by Zelensky, going to the top of *KVK* again, and, having
reached it, saying "Goodbye!" to Maslyakov. Because the
latter not only founded the Club of the Cheerful and Quick-
Witted on Soviet television, but also created a real factory of
stars for Ukrainian and Russian television, the brightest of
whom, to date, was and remains, of course, Zelensky.

After Zelensky's victory in the presidential election,
Maslyakov was asked whether he was proud that the *KVK*
member had become president of Ukraine. He replied:

> There are a lot of remarkable people who were involved
> in this game in their youth. And, of course, many of them
> became distinguished people – they did something useful,
> became famous. But I must admit that, as far as I know,
> none of those who played in the *KVK* improv skit became
> president. Therefore, if not pride, then curiosity is what I
> definitely feel.

And a year later, in May 2020, Maslyakov said: "He is not as
brilliant as *KVK* performer Vova Zelensky."

However, in one of the sketches of the Club of the Cheerful
and Quick-Witted, the captain of Kvartal 95, Zelensky,
offered the president of AMiK (Aleksandr Maslyakov and

Co.) a small bell, saying: "I beg you, Aleksandr Vasilyevich, to take this magic bell. In case you ever face difficulties or find yourself in a hopeless situation, just ring it." "And will we come to the rescue?" someone shouted from the team. "No, but we will know that Aleksandr Vasilyevich remembers us."

Maslyakov is still ringing the bell.

So he does remember Zelensky.

Episode 14

Godfather Rodnyansky

When Zelensky's Kvartal 95 Studio and television life are brought up, just one name is invariably mentioned – that of the current co-owner of the 1+1 TV channel, Ihor Kolomoisky. And this is unfair. Because the main business of Volodymyr Zelensky and his partners would never have started without Oleksandr Rodnyansky – director and producer, and previous co-owner of the channel. It is thanks to him that the most successful entertainment business headed by Zelensky appeared in Ukraine.

In the late 1990s, 1+1, then owned by Rodnyansky and his cousin Borys Fuksman, was one of the most success-ful TV channels in Ukraine. It was at that time – in 1999 – that the Ukrainian Premier League of the Club of the Cheerful and Quick-Witted was founded. It was hosted by the immutable Aleksandr Maslyakov at the Zhovtnevy International Center of Culture and Arts in Kyiv, and the TV version was broadcast on 1+1. Ukrainian, Belarusian, and Russian teams took part in it. Kvartal 95 was among the regular participants in the improv games until 2003. Ten years later, until the end of 2013, the league was determining the winners.

In fact, twice – in 2000 and 2001 – the winners of the Ukrainian *KVK* League were the Three Fat Men team from Khmelnytsky. Popular Ukrainian showmen Oleksandr Pedan and Uncle Zhora (Vadym Mychkovsky) and the then chairman of the Verkhovna Rada of Ukraine, Ruslan Stefanchuk, played for this team.

The artistic director of and actor in *The Diesel Show*, Yegor Krutoholov, actor Andriy Molochny, showman and TV presenter Maks Nelipa, and many other people popular in Ukraine today have come from the Ukrainian *KVK* League.

But let's get back to Kvartal 95. At the end of 2003, Zelensky's team decided to become independent. Zelensky's team's first television show, *Oh! Five 95!*, was filmed in the same Zhovtnevy Palace. It was timed to coincide with the fifth anniversary of Kvartal, although, as Zelensky himself joked from the stage, he had been with the *KVK* for ten years. The program was recorded by two TV channels – 1+1 (Ukraine) and STS (Russia), which at that time was run by Oleksandr Rodnyansky.

The TV show *Oh! Five 95!* was very similar to the *KVK* show, with a number of theatrical skits. There was minimal scenery, provided by the vodka brand 5 Drops. There were frequent onstage announcements from the project sponsors, and salutations to the then president of Ukraine, Leonid Kuchma. The show featured not only Kvartal performers, but also the actors Serhiy Syvokho, Viktor Andriyenko, and Volodymyr Horyansky. Oleksandr Rodnyansky himself took to the stage. "Five years ago, the Kryvyi Rih Kvartal 95 team appeared on this beautiful stage in the Ukrainian *KVK* Open League," the 1+1 general producer began his speech. He continued:

And then we all saw Volodya Zelensky, Lena, Yura, Sasha, and "Yuzik" (Yuriy Koryavchenko). All these wonderful people who went from game to game, beating everyone, but eventually lost. You know, I'm very happy about that today. Because it happened again the next year. Why am I happy? Because sitting here in the front row, I saw tears in the eyes of everyone who played on this stage and played on this team. They really were crying. And then I realized that this was not a game for them. I have also realized this today watching this show. I don't know what the future will hold – a theater, a television program. I can wish for anything. They can do everything! Happy anniversary to you! I want you to come to make the most of everything you can in this life!

Of course, at that moment Oleksandr Rodnyansky had no idea that after a few years the TV show would move from 1+1 to the Inter TV channel, and Volodymyr Zelensky would become his colleague – the general producer of a rival TV channel. With the advent of the TV show, Kvartal 95 Studio quickly gained popularity both in Ukraine and abroad. Zelensky's team was soon performing not only on stage, but also at corporate events. In particular, on the Day of the Journalist, organized by President Viktor Yushchenko's administration in 2006 at the Mariinsky Palace.

And, of course, Rodnyansky had no idea that, after about seven years, Borys Fuksman and he would be persuaded to sell their 1+1 shares to the oligarch Ihor Kolomoisky. And Zelensky's team would return with the *Evening Kvartal* show. Moreover, Rodnyansky could not have predicted that, in 2019, Volodymyr Zelensky would become president of Ukraine and the son of the former general producer of 1+1, Oleksandr Oleksandrovych Rodnyansky, would be appointed chief economic advisor to the cabinet of ministers.

Admittedly, Rodnyansky still had a unique "sixth sense" for the success of projects on television. Yes, the Kvartal players leaving *KVK* split up Alexander Maslyakov's team for good, but this opened the door for Zelensky's team not only into show business but also into politics. It is simply impossible to do the same today. Even with substantial investment. After Zelensky's victory in the presidential election in September 2019, Oleksandr Rodnyansky described him as an "extremely talented man, able to work in a team, and able to clearly and aptly articulate quality statements." He noted that Zelensky managed to become a leader "in a team of pretty talented people" in the program *Crazy Dogs* on Novoe Vremya (New Time) radio.

He predicted Zelensky's future in 2019: "Dreadful days, months, and years await him. And to be honest, you will not envy him, and I am convinced that dislike for him has not even begun. So much will happen, and he will face terrible misunderstandings, and perhaps humiliation, and most likely insults. All this lies ahead for him."

Is Rodnyansky never wrong?

Episode 15
A Scandal in Jurmala

In July 2016, the first "Made in Ukraine" music and stand-up comedy festival took place in Jurmala in Latvia. It was organized by Volodymyr Zelensky and his team. The Kvartal players, together with Ukrainian stars Tina Karol, Jamala, Olha Polyakova, Ruslana, Potap, and the pop group Vremya i Steklo (Time and Glass), entertained the audience at the Latvian resort town for four days.

However, this festival would be remembered by Volodymyr not for the heartfelt reception of the hosts, but rather for the scandal that Kvartal 95 Studio would later get into. In a parody of President Poroshenko, Zelensky compared Ukraine to a porn actress. His clumsy jokes about the loans his country was begging for in the world ended with the phrase: "Ukraine is like an actress in a German porn film ready to take it in any quantity from any side." Jurmala received this joke with laughter, although this may actually have been a defensive reaction caused by an embarrassing situation, given that the popular Ukrainian actor was quite inappropriately joking about his homeland. But Zelensky himself was unaware of any discomfort.

Just two months later, a scandal broke out in Ukraine. Maybe no one would have paid any attention to this performance in Jurmala if it hadn't found its way onto social media networks. People were outraged. "Cheap clown," "Shame and humiliation," "An effing shame," "Sell-out whores for cash" – these were the sweetest words addressed to Kvartal 95 Studio and its frontman. The Kvartal players were reminded about the ebonite rods they joked about during the Revolution of Dignity, and about the rental of films in Russia, and about money from the state budget of the Russian Federation.

A well-known Ukrainian publicist, Vitaliy Portnykov, labeled Zelensky's jokes a product of a modern domestic "sense of humor," low-quality, tasteless, philistine, and shallow. He concluded:

> If people laugh at vulgarity, they must understand that vulgarity does not and cannot have value-added categories and moral boundaries. It is striking that the people who gave Gogol to the world, on whose land all the best satirists and humorists of the twentieth century were born – from Sholom Aleichem to Ostap Vyshnya, from Berezin and Tymoshenko to Zhvanetsky, Ilchenko, and Kartsev – should be proud of Zelensky.

Zelensky was forced to respond to all the allegations on his Facebook page. He said that the joke, which had sparked a heated debate, was not ambiguous. He wrote emotionally:

> It's quite a simple point: it is high time we stopped taking loans, which our children, grandchildren, and those who will live after us have to pay back and will be responsible for everything unpleasant that we are doing now. We are

a proud nation, not beggars. That's all. There is no other meaning here. This is a joke about the actions of our top officials, our government, not about the people or about our country. So you'd better stop pretending to be cultural archaeologists digging for something that is not there and that will never be in the work of Kvartal. We love our country and fight for its freedom, for freedom of speech and thought in every show, every second. Not everything is smooth, guys, not everything is easy, but please don't buy political bullshit that corrupt and petty people write on someone else's order. They cannot be called people either. You are above that. We are above that. Don't let yourself be fooled and fed with this lie. He who calls you a scumbag is either a scumbag himself or is trying to attract our attention. Anyone who calls us a money whore is either a superficial person or a puppet in someone's fat hands.

We are Kvartal! We are patriots! And who are they? You have known us for twenty years! It's quite a long time, isn't it?

After the scandal in Jurmala, Kvartal 95 Studio withdrew its application for making a pitch to the State Cinema of Ukraine for a total of 50 million hryvnias (about $1.7 million). With these funds, Zelensky's team was intending to make a feature film, *Servant of the People*, and a cartoon, *Gulliver's Return*. These projects were put on hold. At the same time, in September 2016, it became known that the film *Eight Best Dates* was a co-production of Ukraine and Russia. When the film was released, Kvartal 95 Studio did not reveal this fact.

Nevertheless, this scandal in Jurmala proved that every word uttered from the stage by the Kvartal players and their frontman began to affect Ukrainian politics. Who knows, maybe this story finally convinced Zelensky to run for president. The show business stage was getting too small for him. He probably understood that he had already crossed the line when his jokes and projects no longer affected hundreds of thousands, but, rather, tens of millions of Ukrainians.

Episode 16

The Family of Kvartal 95

"No to nepotism and friends in power!" This is the slogan that Volodymyr Zelensky took into the 2019 presidential election. He believed that the delegation of power to relatives and friends hindered his main opponent, Petro Poroshenko.

The fifth president of Ukraine, Poroshenko paid a high price for having on his staff his army friend Ihor Kononenko and former business partner Oleh Hladkovsky. With his "favorite friends," he became extremely vulnerable in the final phases of the election campaign. Poroshenko had no cards left to play.

Zelensky swore that, with his coming to power, neither his friends nor his "kumy" (cronies or really close buddies) would rule the country. Only transparent appointments, only social mobility, only the best and most talented would be in power.

Back in 2017, as the artistic director of Kvartal 95 Studio, he pointedly confronted the SBU and those who banned the *In-laws* TV series: "If anyone doesn't like the word 'in-laws' and prefers the word 'kumy,' they'd better do away with their 'kumivstvo' [nepotism] first, and then fight with our *In-laws.*"

In April 2019, already a presidential candidate, Zelensky promised journalists on the Schemes: Corruption in Details program: "Don't worry. There will be no nepotism!" However, he did not fulfill his promise.

A month after winning the election, Zelensky appointed his childhood friend and business partner Ivan Bakanov as deputy head, and later as head, of the security service of Ukraine. Representatives of the creative department of Kvartal 95 Studio were transferred to the Office of the President and to the Verkhovna Rada. "Kumy" also turned up in positions of power – the head of the Office of the President Andriy Yermak and one of the leaders of the Servant of the People Party Mykola Tyshchenko.

In short, Zelensky did not keep his election promise. Indeed, a year after his election, the Poroshenko Family was replaced by the Zelensky Family – or, more precisely, by Kvartal 95 Studio.

The former prosecutor general, Ruslan Ryaboshapka, told me how Zelensky had wanted to appoint a lawyer from Kvartal 95 Studio, Serhiy Ionushys, as his first deputy. Ryaboshapka recalls:

> The discussion was very long and difficult, and he never ended up becoming my first deputy. Many people close to the president wanted to have their own people in the prosecutor's office at the level of deputy prosecutors and at the regional level, which also failed. In addition, there were, and are, many people who would go up to the president and sell him a completely different vision of what we are doing. In fact, the large number of such backstage enemies has altered Zelensky's views on what we do in the prosecutor's office;

his perception of what we are doing and what is happening in the country in general has changed.

So, what did the Zelensky Family look like after his election as president?

- Volodymyr Zelensky, president of Ukraine, former artistic director of Kvartal 95 Studio;
- Ivan Bakanov, head of the SBU, a childhood friend of Zelensky, ex-founder of Kvartal 95 LLC;
- Iryna Borzova, people's deputy, Servant of the People Party, whose father Naum Borulya was Zelensky's partner in the show *League of Laughter*;
- Serhiy Borzov, Iryna Borzova's husband, former head of the state administration, head of the Vinnytsia ODA;
- Vladyslav Bukharev, advisor to the minister of internal affairs, a longtime friend of Volodymyr Zelensky, former head of the Foreign Intelligence Service and former first deputy head of the SBU; it is said that Vladyslav Bukharev and Zelensky's friend Yevhen Koshovy are "kumy";
- Volodymyr Voronov, people's deputy, collaborated with "Kvartal-Concert";
- Olexandr Gogilashvili, an acquaintance of Zelensky, deputy minister of internal affairs;
- Roman Hryshchuk, people's deputy, ex-head of the studio "Mamakhohotala" (mama-was-laughing-out-loud);
- Oleksandr Zavitnevych, people's deputy, Servant of the People Party, chairman of the Verkhovna Rada Committee on National Security, Defense and Intelligence, husband of Volodymyr Zelensky's classmate Natalia Zavitnevych;
- Andriy Yermak, head of the Office of the President (the Yermak Law Firm provided services to Kvartal 95 Studio);
- Oleksandr Kabanov, people's deputy, Servant of the People Party, ex-screenwriter at the Kvartal 95 Studio;
- Oleksandr Kachura, people's deputy, Servant of the

People Party (the Kachura Law Firm provided services to Kvartal 95 Studio);

• Volodymyr Kyiashko, Olena Zelensky's father, previously managed the companies LLC Kryvorizhmonolitbud and LLC Technoimpulse, assistant to Oleh Bondarenko, a people's deputy on a voluntary basis;

• Yuriy Koryavchenkov, people's deputy, Servant of the People Party, former actor and former administrative director of Kvartal 95 Studio;

• Yuriy Kostyuk, deputy head of the Office of the President, former creative producer and screenwriter at Kvartal 95 Studio;

• Ihor Kryvosheev, people's deputy, showman, former player in the *League of Laughter*;

• Olexandr Pashkov, director of the department of strategic intelligence at the ministry of defense, husband of the chief accountant of Kvartal 95 Studio;

• Iryna Pobedonostseva, chief consultant of the information policy directorate at the Office of the President of Ukraine, former director of development of Kvartal 95 Studio;

• Olha Rudenko, people's deputy, Servant of the People Party, ex-employee of the press service of Kvartal 95 Studio;

• Tetyana Rudenko, member of the National Council on Television and Radio Broadcasting, ex-head of the press service of Kvartal 95 Studio;

• Serhiy Sivokho, former creative producer of Kvartal 95 Studio, ex-advisor to the secretary of the National Security and Defense Council;

• Oleksandr Skichko, head of the Cherkasy ODA, former actor and showman;

• Valery Sterniychuk, people's deputy, ex-head of the Student's League of Laughter in Volyn;

- Ruslan Stefanchuk, parliamentary speaker, friend of Volodymyr Zelensky since *KVK* times, member of the Three Fat Men team (Khmelnytsky);
- Mykola Stefanchuk, brother of the parliamentary speaker, people's deputy, Servant of the People Party;
- Mykola Tyshchenko, people's deputy, Servant of the People Party, Andriy Yermak's godfather and a longtime friend of Zelensky;
- Maksym Tkachenko, people's deputy, advisor to the secretary of the National Security and Defense Council, former general director of Kvartal-Concert;
- Olena Khomenko, people's deputy, former digital director of Kvartal 95 Studio;
- Serhiy Shefir, first aide to the president of Ukraine, Zelensky's business partner at Kvartal 95 Studio.

Sure enough, one can say that President Zelensky enjoyed a high level of trust from Ukrainian society, and this is what allowed him to choose those with whom to work. In part, this is correct. However, what about "kumy"/brothers/partners? How come a *League of Laughter* graduate or a *KVK* member has an advantage over a Yale or a Harvard graduate? Where are the promised equalities of opportunity and upward social mobility?

The answers, like the questions, are rhetorical. At least under the almost absolute power of Zelensky in Ukraine.

Family.

Partners.

"Kumy."

Friends.

Zelensky's path resembled that of his predecessors. With all the associated risks and consequences.

Episode 17

The Kadyrov Ordeal

On October 6, 2014, on the talk show *Chysto NEWS* (Purely the NEWS) hosted by Volodymyr Zelensky, the Kvartal comedians made fun of Ramzan Kadyrov (head of the Chechen Republic). More precisely, Zelensky recited a commentary to a video in which he said the Chechen leader had reacted to the demolition of the monument to Lenin in Kharkiv.

"Lenin was overthrown. We've lived for eighty years and have never seen anything like it. Fascists, Banderites,"[1] says the voiceover, and in the video Kadyrov wipes away tears. Kvartal 95 Studio used a video recording of a real pensioner crying at the sight of a fallen monument.

Zelensky had to pay a high price for this nineteen-second joke on *Chysto NEWS*. After the video was aired, the Kadyrovites began demanding apologies; it turned out that the video had been shot at a memorial service for the Chechen leader's father, who died on May 9, 2004. Russian

---

[1] The Russian pejorative term for extreme Ukrainian nationalists, which comes from the name of Ukrainian nationalist WWII leader Stepan Bandera (1909–59).

State Duma Deputy Shasmail Saraliyev advised Zelensky to "prepare for his own burial."

Zelensky was forced to immediately apologize publicly for the video. He did so on October 9. However, he apologized not to Kadyrov himself, but to the entire Muslim world, saying:

> Honestly, I didn't know that this video had anything to do with a funeral. At first there was limited information. Regardless of the politician in question – be it Mr. Kadyrov, Putin, or Poroshenko – such things should simply not be joked about. If I did so, then I say "I beg your pardon." And even if it wasn't a funeral, but a sacred Muslim occasion, I respect all religions, I would never laugh at the sacred. That's why I say: "I apologize to everyone I offended, to all Muslims."

Later, however, he clarified that he did not apologize personally to Ramzan Kadyrov.

According to another information source, Zelensky was still trying to resolve the conflict with the Chechen leader through the ministry of internal affairs. The issue was allegedly settled as a result of organized talks between Ukrainian law-enforcement officers and Chechen colleagues. Apparently, it was agreed that Zelensky would fly to Chechnya together with Yuriy Yerinyak, who allegedly had connections in the criminal world; but the artistic director of Kvartal 95 Studio never flew to Grozny. Yerinyak had to apologize to the Kadyrovites himself. At the same time, in December 2014, a bottle containing an incendiary mixture was thrown into Zelensky's Range Rover near the National Palace of the Arts "Ukraina." The frontman of Kvartal didn't comment on the attempted arson regarding his car.

Instead, Zelensky's wife Olena later told reporters that

they had to hire private security guards after receiving threats against her husband from the Kadyrovites. "We still don't know if the threat was real or if law-enforcement officers tried to scare us with stories that Chechen criminals were coming to Kyiv to hunt us down," Olena told *The Daily Beast* in May 2019.

In fact, in December 2014, Ramzan Kadyrov instructed law-enforcement officers and special forces of the republic to initiate criminal proceedings against the people's deputies of Ukraine, Yuriy Bereza, Ihor Mosiychuk, and Andriy Levus, for commenting on the events in Grozny. Moreover, the Chechen leader ordered that these three, together with Isa Munayev, be detained and brought to Chechnya. Meanwhile, in the Chechen capital on December 5, 2014, Ichkerian soldiers killed seventy Kadyrovites. After threats from the Chechen leader against Ukrainian deputies, the Ukrainian ministry of internal affairs launched criminal proceedings based on this fact.

If anyone thinks that the story of Ramzan Kadyrov and Volodymyr Zelensky is over, they are very wrong.

In December 2018, a week before Zelensky announced his intention to run for president, the journalist Dmytro Gordon brought up the issue of Kadyrov and Zelensky's apology. The artistic director of Kvartal 95 Studio explained the story of 2014 as follows:

> On our program *Chysto NEWS* there was a video, which I didn't see since I was not in charge of this program then, another group was. It wasn't even about him; there was a video clip, and this shot of Ramzan Kadyrov's crying got into that clip. I received a phone call in which I was asked how, in my opinion, the Muslim world would react. I replied that I did not know what it was about, but I promised to look into the matter. Because religion is a very delicate issue.

On July 19, 2020, the Chechen leader posted Zelensky's response in his Telegram channel and called on Zelensky to apologize to him once again. He wrote:

> Once I used to know Zelensky as a man who, having admitted his guilt, was noble enough to apologize. It was the behavior of a decent man. But why now, after apologies have been accepted, try to pretend something else, invent excuses, whitewash, and boost yourself? Now, having won power as president of Ukraine, you are inventing new versions of your apologies at every stage. You will have to be firm in your position and confirm your apologies. If not, you will have to confront me not as head of the Republic, but as the son of the first leader of the Chechen Republic, the hero of Russia Akhmat-Haji Kadyrov, whose memory you have offended!

He also asked Zelensky why he wouldn't call Putin and announce that he was ending the "civil war in the east." To save a trip, so to speak.

In response, the Office of the President of Ukraine claimed that it made no sense to comment on or discuss the Chechen leader's statement.

On February 14, 2022, Kadyrov again publicly addressed Zelensky, urging him to implement the Minsk agreements. In that way, Kadyrov said, Ukraine could avoid war with Russia. However, Zelensky ignored Kadyrov's appeal. Furthermore, at the start of the Kremlin's hostilities on Ukrainian soil, the Ukrainian special services stated publicly that it was the Kadyrovites who were preparing to assassinate Zelensky, but they were defeated near Kyiv. The Chechen leader, on the other hand, called on Zelensky to resign and let the former Ukrainian president, Viktor Yanukovych, who fled to Russia in February 2014, take over the presidency.

Episode 18

Ebonite Rods

In winter 2013–14, Kvartal 95 Studio cracked a lot of jokes about the Maidan (Independence Square) protests against the Yanukovych government. In the New Year show, Zelensky's team ridiculed President Yanukovych and Prime Minister Viktor Azarov. They also mocked the protesters and opposition leaders. Kvartal performers were convinced that the country, just like them, would not accept street democracy. Because if they hadn't done this, there probably wouldn't have been a joke about ebonite rods, which Zelensky is still being reminded of. And how could one not mention it when people were being beaten up and killed in the center of the Ukrainian capital during the Revolution of Dignity, while Yevhen Koshovy, who played the part of the ex-mayor of Kyiv Leonid Chernovetsky, and Oleksandr Pikalov, who performed the role of ex-president Viktor Yanukovych, were joking about the beating of Maidan participants during one of Kvartal's concerts?

"*Koshovy*: Viktor Fedorovych, I have a question about physics. If the Berkut [special police] forces were given ebonite rods and the protesters were dressed in woolen clothing, would we be able to get electricity?"

It is clear that both in 2004 and in 2014, Volodymyr Zelensky and his team were nowhere near the Maidan in Kyiv. Most of the participants in Kvartal 95 Studio grew up in Kryvyi Rih or in eastern Ukraine. The team's frontmen began their careers in Moscow. For them, questions of language, faith, and identity have never been an issue. So it is obvious that there were no Kvartal performers on the Maidan either. In addition, they had always felt at ease under different administrations – under Presidents Kuchma, Yushchenko, and Yanukovych. As they say, it was nothing personal, just business.

In spring 2014, when Russia had already annexed Crimea and inspired pro-Russian rallies in eastern Ukraine, Kvartal 95 Studio toured the Donbas. On April 17, the very day that Volodymyr Rybak, a deputy of the city council, was abducted and brutally killed by pro-Russian forces in Horlivka, Zelensky's team staged a concert in the city. They did perform. And although you won't be able to find any video of the concert online (apparently, they were removed during the 2019 presidential election), which would have proven it, there are nevertheless witnesses to the event.

That day, Yevhen Koshovy and Volodymyr Zelensky gave an interview to a local TV channel. The conversation began with the question: "Weren't you afraid to go to the east given the current turbulent situation?" To which Zelensky replied that the team did not consider canceling the show because the audience was ready and waiting for them, adding: "The best thing we can do for Ukraine now is to exert maximum effort to unite the country and stir up those in power so that they work and defend the country and its borders; it is very important."

So, once again.

As pro-Russian forces were brutally killing Rybak in Horlivka, Zelensky continued to talk about unification of the country and the need to shake up the Ukrainian government as much as possible.

Five years later, on April 19, 2019, Volodymyr Rybak's widow Olena would remind Zelensky of what happened in Horlivka. On her Facebook page, she wrote about how the Kvartal show took place just 500 meters from the place where her husband was abducted:

My husband was "taken" near the theater, as he probably wanted to get lost in the crowd, but did not have time. My husband risked his own life, mine, and the lives of our children. Kvartal 95 arrived to shake up the government. Wasn't it enough that separatists had already been stirring it up for two months? Did Kvartal have to join in? They sang a song about Crimea. And the Donbas didn't care a bit. They opposed Kyiv. Crimea was taken away from Kyiv not from them, and they would continue going on vacations to Crimea as they used to do before. Kvartal mostly ridiculed the Ukrainian authorities, especially Klitschko [the world champion boxer Vitaliy, and Mayor of Kyiv], who constantly exalted Ukraine, and whose name is already inscribed in history.

And what have you, Mr. Zelensky, done for Ukraine? You performed shows for the military, didn't you? Well, it's safer than serving in the army yourself . . .

I have a question, how did you get permission to perform in Horlivka on April 17, 2014, when all the pro-Ukrainians were in hiding and leaving the city?

Olena Rybak asked Zelensky this question. However, she never received an answer.

Of course, after the ebonite rods incident, the tour of already semi-captured cities of the Donbas, and with the beginning of Russian aggression, Zelensky's team realized that it could no longer keep walking on such thin ice. It was necessary to decide whose side to take. Trips to the frontline of the war in the Donbas, giving performances for the Ukrainian military, and volunteer assistance to the army seem to have clarified the political stance of Kvartal 95. In this way, at least, the Kvartal performers apologized for their inappropriate jokes about Ukrainian patriots. But Zelensky's ebonite rods are unlikely to be forgotten. His opponents keep reminding him of the story.

Episode 19

Zelensky's Double

On October 9, 2018, political strategist Dmytro Razumkov appeared at Volodymyr Zelensky's campaign headquarters.

By an irony of fate, six months earlier Razumkov had publicly doubted that a Ukrainian version of Emmanuel Macron would emerge in Ukraine, a man who would win the presidential election without appreciable support from a national party.

Conversely, Roman Bezsmertny, a politician and one of the participants in the 2019 presidential race, was convinced that the Ukrainian state was indeed anticipating its own Macron. He spoke about this on air in 2018 and 2019:

> Why did I talk about Macron and Ukrainian Macronisms during Poroshenko's presidency? The reason for this was not some kind of prophecy or sorcery, the possibility or ability to predict, but the activities of Poroshenko himself. Now, against the background of the "feats" of Zelensky and his team, we forget about such things and do not pay tribute to them. But in fact, and I am absolutely convinced of this,

the post-Yanukovych period and Poroshenko's own activities necessitated what I called "a Macron." Because there
has to be a well-known person in society destined to crush
the political system. And, in fact, this is what is happening.
Macron did not belong to any political party. Moreover,
he maneuvered between political forces and effectively
destroyed the existing political system. That's what Zelensky
has done. He actually destroyed the political system. But
why doesn't Zelensky's case exactly coincide? Macron was a
man of the system in a state with strong institutions. If you
consider the institutions of a democratic society or the institutions of the state, they are strong. And in the Ukrainian
context, the activities of the fifth president required just
such a figure. Because it must be clearly stated that Petro
Poroshenko took very seriously the fact that certain institutions should either be liquidated or reorganized. And the
newly created ones could not function at full capacity. Take,
for example, the Office of the Prosecutor General itself,
which has become completely impotent; instead, agencies
of all sorts – DBR, NAZK [National Agency on Corruption
Prevention], NABU [National Anti-Corruption Bureau of
Ukraine], and the Anti-Corruption Court – have been created, none of which has been able to operate effectively.

But Macron's views, position, and philosophy are not just
those of Emmanuel Macron. A group of scholars proposed
this policy; it is a serious national philosophy based on the
French school of philosophy, the school of economics, the
school of state development, the political school, and so on.
It was clear that Ukraine needed similar approaches. But,
unfortunately, Zelensky himself as a person is not a Macron,
and, moreover, nor are the people around him.

However, back to Razumkov. If in April 2018, as an ana-
lyst, he was wrong in his predictions about the Ukrainian

Macron, then, in October 2019, he drew his lucky ticket, de facto becoming the face of Volodymyr Zelensky's election campaign.

Razumkov himself claims to have joined the team of the sixth president of Ukraine thanks to Ivan Bakanov. The story goes something like this: Razumkov and Bakanov had common friends who brought them together. And this led to an acquaintance with Zelensky, and, shortly afterward, a work appearance at the campaign headquarters. Obviously, though, nothing was as simple as Dmytro Razumkov himself tries to present it. After all, he can hardly be called a random person in Ukrainian politics. He is the son of the former first aide to the then president of Ukraine, Leonid Kuchma. And it seems that his name itself should suffice to lead him into politics, because most of those who knew his father are still active players in the life of the country.

It must be said that Oleksandr Razumkov was a prominent and influential figure during the term of the second president of Ukraine. He graduated from the faculty of international relations at the Taras Shevchenko State University of Kyiv. He began his career in the regional committee of the Komsomol (Communist Youth League) of the Dnipropetrovsk Region, where he met Serhiy Tihipko. As it happens, Oleksandr Turchynov (former secretary of the RNBO) also started his Komsomol career there. This was followed by work in the central committee of the LKSMU (Leninist Communist Union of Ukrainian Youth) and the Verkhovna Rada's Commission on Youth Affairs.

In 1994, the elder Razumkov joined the headquarters of the then-presidential candidate Leonid Kuchma, and, after the election, became his chief of staff. However, he didn't enjoy this status for long – as a result of conflicts with the then head of the Office of the President Dmytro Tabachnyk, he was forced to resign. He founded his own

Razumkov Center for Political and Economic Research, and later became deputy secretary of the RNBO, which oversaw Russo-Ukrainian matters in the country's foreign policy. In fact, in 1997, on the recommendation of Razumkov, Serhiy Tihipko was appointed deputy minister of economic affairs in Pavlo Lazarenko's government. "The marketing-theorist was replaced by the marketing-practitioner," was Oleksandr Razumkov's comment on the replacement of Viktor Pynzenyk by Serhiy Tihipko.

The elder Razumkov lived a short life. At the age of 40, he died of an incurable disease. By that time, he had already left Dmytro's mother, the famous actress Nataliya Kudrya, and had started another family in a civil marriage with journalist Yuliya Mostova, with whom he had a son Hlib, who, by the way, was later adopted by Yuliya's next husband, ex-minister of defense Anatoliy Hrytsenko.

Time would pass, and Dmytro ended up following in his father's footsteps. Like the elder Razumkov, he graduated from the Kyiv Institute of International Relations, which was established along the lines of the faculty of international relations. Like his father, he took his first steps in politics. Not in the Komsomol, of which there would be no trace left, but in the Party of Regions, which he joined after his opposition to President Yushchenko. Like his father, he was close to Serhiy Tihipko, by then an influential, wealthy man who would dream of the presidency. And like his father, was on the team of the presidential candidate who would win the election. However, it wouldn't be Tihipko.

It turned out later that everything that had happened before 2018 was just a training session for Dmytro Razumkov. He left the Party of Regions in 2010 – following Viktor Yanukovych's victory in the presidential election. He participated in the 2010 campaign, which resulted in an unexpected third place for Serhiy Tihipko, who was

appointed deputy prime minister in Mykola Azarov's government, and which led to the foundation of and merger
between the Sylna Ukraina (A Strong Ukraine) Party and the
Party of Regions. However, within two years Razumkov and
Tihipko had parted company – the former started working as an advisor to the head of the Kirovohrad Regional
State Administration, Andriy Nikolayenko, and the latter
returned to big business.

Political strategist Kost Bondarenko, who worked with
Tihipko's Sylna Ukraina Party, says he does not remember
the younger Razumkov in Tihipko's party election campaign. "Maybe he was somewhere, of course, but probably
playing a secondary or tertiary role," Bondarenko recalls.

After turning up at Zelensky's headquarters, Dmytro
Razumkov became one of the central media figures in the
election campaign. An attractive, intelligent, and discreet
political strategist, he played the role of backup to the presidential candidate; he conducted discussions on his behalf on
TV channels; and he complemented his image. Razumkov
spoke only Russian then, explaining this as follows: "As
long as there is Russian aggression, as long as the Russian
state wants to protect the Russian-speaking population, I
use only Russian during broadcasts. Because I don't think
it's necessary to have tanks with machine guns and 'little
green men'[1] to protect me as part of the Russian-speaking
population." However, this explanation was, to put it mildly,
strange. More precisely, Russian clearly was and remains
Razumkov's main language of communication.

Until April 2019, Zelensky avoided public debates
with his main opponent Petro Poroshenko and refused
to participate in TV shows except for a few broadcasts of

---

[1] What Ukrainians called the Russian troops in unmarked uniforms who
took over Crimea in 2014.

Pravo na Vladu (The Right to Power) on the 1+1 channel. Consequently, Razumkov had to show up in the right places. More precisely, as a political strategist he worked on shaping the image of the future president. And Razumkov did it, by his own admission, on a voluntary basis. He would later say that there was no job contract or any remuneration at the time. Razumkov simply played on the team he wanted to win.

After Zelensky's victory in the presidential election, everyone was looking forward to finding out which office Dmytro Razumkov would hold. But in May 2019, despite all expectations, he had no appointment. Instead, he headed the Servant of the People Party, which he led to early parliamentary elections. He became the face of a new political force for which Ukrainians had high hopes.

There was Razumkov in a field, Razumkov at a factory, Razumkov among students, Razumkov at a construction site.

Razumkov, coming out from under the shadow of Zelensky, tried to make up for his time in the political "underground." The role of backup did not suit him very well. Like any backup singer, he dreamed of a solo political career.

Two months later, the presidential party won a landslide victory, and three years later, 35-year-old Dmytro Razumkov became speaker of the Verkhovna Rada, meaning, in effect, that he was second in the power structure of the country, because, according to the Constitution, if, under any circumstances, the president is unable to perform his duties, the parliamentary speaker becomes the interim leader. Recall how, in 2014, after Viktor Yanukovych's flight from Ukraine, the speaker of the Verkhovna Rada Oleksandr Turchynov became interim president. So Razumkov advanced one step closer to the presidency.

Yes, Razumkov was forced to pay verbal obeisances to Zelensky. Yes, his career did depend on the single-party majority formed by the presidential Servant of the People Party. Yes, he played on Zelensky's team. Yes, he sometimes made strange political statements, such as, for example, concerning the need to revise the language law. However, Razumkov increasingly began to feel his political power, opposing Zelensky's initiatives at a meeting of the Security and Defense Council. And after a while he was no longer perceived as Zelensky's "talking head" or as the son of Oleksandr Razumkov. The younger Razumkov realized that he could not only be a backup presidential candidate, but he could also lead the state. Zelensky also understood this. On October 7, 2021, the majority voted to remove Razumkov from the post of speaker. Since then, he has been a politician "on the prowl for a mate," a leader of the Rozumna Polityka (Smart Politics) project, and an opponent of Zelensky. Of course, with pretensions to the presidency. Like Zelensky had in 2019.

On November 27, 2021, Razumkov announced that he would run for president of Ukraine.

Episode 20

Zelensky's Ceremonial General

A week after his inauguration on May 28, 2019, Volodymyr Zelensky restored Ukrainian citizenship to Mikheil Saakashvili (Georgia's former president). Ukraine's new president was convinced that his predecessor (Petro Poroshenko) had unfairly treated the former leader of Georgia. Zelensky probably wanted Saakashvili's return to be seen as a symbol of the restoration of justice after the era of Poroshenko's "hucksterism." Saakashvili, who had been deported to Poland from Ukraine with a sack over his head, felt really triumphant following his return to Ukraine.

In 2015, when Saakashvili first received Ukrainian citizenship and became head of Odesa's ODA, Poroshenko sang the praises of Georgia's former president and celebrated their many years of friendship. Poroshenko and Saakashvili had both studied in the faculty of international relations at Kyiv State University, almost at the same time (incidentally, the current head of the Office of the President, Andriy Yermak, graduated from the same faculty just a few years later). In 2004, Poroshenko and Saakashvili both took the side of the Orange Revolution, and became friends with

President Viktor Yushchenko, who even became godfather to Saakashvili's younger son Nikolaz.[1] And in 2014, following the Revolution of Dignity, Saakashvili lent his support to Poroshenko during the presidential race.

It seemed that there would be no end to the friendship between the two men. Certainly, no one could have imagined that Saakashvili would begin publicly to disparage Poroshenko using the derogatory word "huckster," and to call on Ukrainians to overthrow his former friend. Poroshenko in response would deprive Saakashvili of his Ukrainian passport and deport him. But nonetheless this is what happened.

Saakashvili's hot temper, as well as his conflicts with practically the entire ruling class of Ukraine at the time, quickly turned the former Georgian president into a political freak, who even took flight along the rooftops of buildings in Kyiv to escape from Ukrainian security agents.

Poroshenko's presidency was obviously one of the most complex and dramatic times in Mikheil Saakashvili's political career. He faced charges of plotting a government coup, confinement in jail, and deportation to Poland. As a result, one of the authors of the "Georgian miracle" (Saakashvili), whom Poroshenko, like Zelensky, wanted to make a ceremonial general for Ukrainian reforms, was forced to spend a certain amount of time in Europe.

It should be noted that, at the end of 2017, Prosecutor General Yuriy Lutsenko announced from the rostrum of the Verkhovna Rada that Mikheil Saakashvili and his comrades-in-arms were preparing a government coup in Ukraine funded by the oligarch Serhiy Kurchenko. According to the HPU (Office of the Prosecutor General), Saakashvili's protest

---

[1] In Ukrainian culture, when someone becomes a "kum" or "kuma" (godparent), s/he becomes almost as close as a blood relative.

actions were financed by Russia. But then, according to the court's ruling, one of Saakashvili's allies, Severion Dangadze, was detained, albeit for a short time, and Saakashvili himself became one of those who were preparing their revenge in Ukraine.

Right after Saakashvili regained his Ukrainian citizenship, Yuriy Lutsenko publicly reiterated that he considered, and still considers, the former president of Georgia to be a traitor to Ukraine. However, after the latter's arrival in Kyiv by air, the HPU took no action against him.

After having his passport, complete with the Ukrainian gold trident, restored in 2019, Saakashvili set off for Odesa, where he had been head of the ODA back in the time of Poroshenko. There, as was expected, he was supposed to take part in the October 2020 mayoral election, with Zelensky's support. However, the internal disruptions that overwhelmed Zelensky's team in winter 2020 forced him to return to Kyiv. Oleksiy Honcharuk's resignation from the post of prime minister of Ukraine and the rise of Denys Shmygal to that position demanded radical actions from the Servant of the People Party. One of them was the recruitment of Saakashvili to the team of the sixth president.

However, the suggestion that he take up the post of deputy prime minister for economic reforms, which was apparently presented to Saakashvili on behalf of Zelensky, remained unrealized. Saakashvili rushed to Parliament to lend his support to the presidential majority, but there were insufficient votes to appoint him to the government. Yes indeed. The very same Saakashvili, who had cursed the "hucksterism" of Poroshenko in all kinds of ways and who constantly exhibited his Caucasus pride, suddenly calmly "swallowed" the fact that he was "knocked out" as deputy prime minister. Incidentally, Georgia also opposed

Saakashvili's appointment to the Ukrainian government and threatened to recall its ambassador from Kyiv.

On May 7, 2020, Zelensky appointed Saakashvili as head of the Supreme Coordinating Committee of the National Reform Council, an advisory body that had been set up under Poroshenko. It was a structure that carried no state authority. The former president of Georgia was given the role of ceremonial advocate for Zelensky's reforms. This position certainly involved great media opportunities, but nothing more than that.

Saakashvili said he would never quarrel with Zelensky. According to him, it was only their enemies who expected this. But, as they say, "never say 'never'." Besides, Zelensky's Ukraine was not very different from Poroshenko's, which Saakashvili had opposed so vehemently. These were all the same "masters of the country" – the oligarchs Ihor Kolomoisky, Rinat Akhmetov, and Viktor Pinchuk, whom the former president of Georgia had publicly and sharply criticized. This was the very same system of government, built on bribery and "hucksterism," that had so irritated, and continued to irritate, Saakashvili.

Saakashvili could have taken on the role of player-coach on Zelensky's team. But he was not permitted to do so.

In August 2020, Saakashvili harshly criticized the several unsuccessful staff changes made at the customs office by Zelensky's team. And on August 27, he released a video in which he announced he would return to Georgia after seven years away from the country. Saakashvili promised to return home after the parliamentary elections and lead the opposition party in Georgia, the United National Movement. He clarified that "wherever he is, he will always be a faithful son of two friendly countries – Georgia and Ukraine." In Tbilisi, criminal cases against Saakashvili resurfaced and he was imprisoned.

Political strategist Serhiy Haidai is convinced that Saakashvili's departure from Ukrainian politics testified to just one thing: he doesn't believe in the strength of Zelensky. As he put it: "He took a break [from Ukrainian politics] in fact, because of Zelensky. This is not so much an entrance into Georgian politics as a departure from Zelensky. He lost faith in the idea that Zelensky would ever give him the opportunity to become prime minister, to create a team."

In fall 2021, Saakashvili returned illegally to Georgia to support his allies. He was arrested there on old charges. All Zelensky's attempts to influence officials in Tbilisi to free Saakashvili from jail as a citizen of Ukraine have been unsuccessful. Saakashvili remains in prison.

Episode 21

Zelensky's Shefir Brothers

The year 1995 was a decisive one for Volodymyr Zelensky.

As a 17-year-old teenager, he liked the theater and the *KVK*. His father wanted his son to have a strong education and a job with good prospects. However, it is now obvious that the country would hardly have heard about Zelensky if he had become an engineer, gone into the military, or became a doctor. And who knows whether he would be satisfied with his life if everything had turned out differently.

That year a meeting took place in Zelensky's life that forever ended his doubts about what he should become. In Kryvyi Rih he met two brothers – Borys and Serhiy Shefir. They were nearly twice his age. At the time, the former was 35 years old, the latter 31. Their father, Nakhman Meilakhovych Shefir, had fought in World War II and, as Serhiy Shefir himself admitted, fought against the Banderites[1] after the war in western Ukraine; he was

---

[1] The followers of Stepan Bandera, leader of the Organization of Ukrainian Nationalists during and after WWII.

also an inventor. Like Zelensky's father, he dreamed that his boys would become someone in their lives. Serhiy and Borys both graduated from the Kryvyi Rih Mining Institute. However, their father surely had no idea that, instead of ore, his sons would mine show business stars, the first of whom would be Volodymyr Zelensky.

When they met Zelensky, Serhiy and Borys were already part of the *KVK* Kryvyi Rih Tramps and the Zaporizhzhya–Kryvyi Rih–Transit teams. And since there was an entire league of the *KVK* in their hometown, it was impossible not to cross paths with Volodymyr Zelensky. They first invited the young man to do dance numbers for Transit. Two years later, in 1997, it was this team that battled for the championship with the New Armenians in the *KVK* finals in Moscow. And another year later, some members of Transit, including Zelensky and the Shefirs, created a new team, Kvartal 95, which was represented at the *KVK* festival in Sochi.

Together with the Shefirs, Zelensky experienced the first upward swings in his stellar career, because it was the brothers who helped him get acclimated to Moscow. The three of them rented a one-room apartment in Mytishchi and worked for Aleksandr Maslyakov's AMiK. The brothers not only worked on Kvartal 95, but also wrote scripts for the teams of *KVK* Minsk, the Makhachkala Tramps, the National Team of the Twentieth Century, and the National Team of the Twenty-First Century.

It turned out that 2003 was a critical year for the trio. That year, the Shefir brothers and Zelensky, with the support of Oleksandr Rodnyansky, decided to create the company Kvartal 95 Studio. Then there was a break with Maslyakov. Then they moved from Moscow to Kyiv. That marked the start of a collaboration with the 1+1 TV channel, and then with the Inter TV channel. It was also the start of filmmaking. *Food is Served, Professor Kingpin, The In-laws, Eight First Dates,* and others.

Over the course of the next twenty-five years, the three friends – and later business partners – became the founders of the successful Kvartal 95 company. In 2019, they converted their influence into the presidency for Volodymyr Zelensky. I am sure that if someone had told these three young men in 1995 that one of them would become president of Ukraine, they would have thought that person insane. But it happened. After the inauguration of the sixth president, Borys Shefir remained in charge of Kvartal 95, and his younger brother Serhiy became the first assistant to the head of state, and it was predicted he would take up the position of the head of the Office of the President. Serhiy said in an interview with the LB.ua website that his main task under President Zelensky was to maintain the latter's humanity in politics.

Former head of the Office of the President Andriy Bohdan called Serhiy Shefir the most trusted person on President Zelensky's staff. "Shefir is nice; he is a mentor to Volodya [Zelensky]. He is probably his most trusted friend. At least he was. He's really nice. I have nothing bad to say about him. You see, there is wisdom in him, but there is an understanding of the algorithm. You understand, he has wisdom. He has reason, wisdom. He is wise. But he is not a bureaucrat; he does not come from that world" – this is how Bohdan characterized him in an interview with the journalist Dmytro Gordon.

I should say that the Shefir brothers have always avoided publicity. And maybe that was the right thing to do. Otherwise, who knows what fate would have befallen Volodymyr Zelensky if Borys Shefir had not publicly spoken out against proposed laws requiring language quotas (of 100 percent Ukrainian content in broadcast media) and called Russian President Vladimir Putin "a smart man with whom one can negotiate" not after, but before the presidential election.

On May 30, 2020, in an interview with the Internet publication *Detector Media*, the elder Shefir brother stated: "My attitude to the war is the way I understand it – it was started to make money on both sides. Everyone made money, only they brought us and you to ruin," adding: "If we really wanted to, we could come to an agreement with them." Emphasizing that, with the change of power in Ukraine, the war will "quiet down," Borys Shefir said:

> What, do they like to fight a war? Do you think Putin is a maniac who likes to shoot at living people? Is he a psychopath? He is an intelligent man. Yes, he has imperial ambitions. But you can come to some kind of agreement. And if not, we'll need to declare a real war. And what happens? We fight with one hand and trade with the other? The desire of at least one side is very important, otherwise there are no prospects for peace.

This was the elder Shefir brother's first and last interview. After this, Zelensky's team was forced to declare that it did not share Borys's position. However, the statement of Zelensky's old friend tells us more than enough to get a sense of the environment in which Zelensky grew up. As the saying goes: tell me who your friend is, and I'll tell you who you are.

The Shefir brothers were and remained close friends with Zelensky and his staff.

To paraphrase a classic phrase: when we say Zelensky, we have in mind the Shefirs; when we say the brothers Shefir, we mean Zelensky.

On September 22, 2021, there was an attempted

assassination of Serhiy Shefir near Kyiv. On his way to the capital, his car was shot at by an unknown assailant. While in New York at a meeting of the UN General Assembly, Zelensky told this story. According to him, they weren't shooting at Shefir, but at the reforms he was carrying out in Ukraine. In particular, changes that would affect the removal of oligarchs from influence on political processes in the government. Zelensky promised that the response of the presidential team to the attempted assassination of Shefir would be strong. However, so far, the perpetrators and the ones who ordered the assassination attempt on the president's chief of staff have not been found.

Episode 22

Kolomoisky's Knife

Legends abound about this person. One of them is that, at a business party, he cut off part of the tie of one of his top managers with a cake knife. As if to say: I know everything about your activities and you should be grateful to me for letting you get away with it. Everyone who knows Kolomoisky speaks about his cruelty and shrewdness in his business affairs. The character himself is quite skeptical about all the rumors about him and says that people who've never seen him in person are the ones who gossip about him.

Zelensky could say a lot about Kolomoisky and his manner of communication, since, for quite a long time, his Kvartal 95 Studio worked closely with the 1+1 TV channel, which is controlled by Kolomoisky. On October 6, 2012, the two companies officially announced plans for cooperation. *Evening Kvartal, Evening Kyiv,* and *Make a Comedian Laugh* began to appear on the 1+1 channel. After six years, and thanks to Kolomoisky's informational resources, Zelensky became a megastar in Ukrainian show business.

According to Kolomoisky, it was Tymur Mindych and Yuriy Borysov who introduced him to the actor in 2008.

But it cannot be said that relations between Kolomoisky and Zelensky have always been trusting and simple, especially with respect to the oligarch's financial terms with Kvartal.

On Kolomoisky's birthday on February 13, 2017, Zelensky, with his friends, the actors of the Kvartal, recorded a video message for him. In it, the actors greeted the birthday boy in a jocular tone and requested that he return at least a small part of a large debt owed by the 1+1 TV channel to Kvartal 95 Studio. When Zelensky heard this, he turned to Kolomoisky: "Ihor Valeriyovych, we congratulate you on your birthday. I wish you the very same as the guys did. Many friends, a long life, health, and grandchildren. I wish that next year everything will be the same as it has been up until now for you. And for us – that at least something will change."

However, despite this appeal to the oligarch, nothing changed for Kvartal in 2018. It was the same the following year. The amount owed by the channel to Kvartal 95 Studio was announced in the press – $4 million.

On July 18, 2019, in an interview with LB.ua, top advisor to the president, Serhiy Shefir, in answer to a question from Sonya Koshkina about whether it was true that TV channel 1+1 owed nearly $7 million to the Kvartal Studio, replied:

> Listen, the situation in the country has not been easy. From 2012 to 2014 – in terms of financial relations – everything was fine for us. But then the war started, and I remember it well: we went to the Dnipro ODA [with Kolomoisky as governor], let's say, with some questions, and at that time the defense plan was being discussed. A helicopter flies in, lands, volunteers unload it, there are wounded, etc. They really stopped the war in Dnipro. Why am I bringing this up? In fact, these were the circumstances in which it was

not so simple to comply with all the previously accepted conditions.

On October 5, 2021 a group of investigative journalists, examining a leaked document about offshore accounts (the Pandora Papers), revealed evidence of Zelensky's involvement with offshore companies. They found that, since 2012, he and his associates had received $40 million from offshore accounts of Kolomoisky's companies from Privatbank.

Zelensky himself confirms that, as a businessman, he used offshore accounts, but he did not launder money through them. In an interview with ICTV on October 17, 2021, the president said:

> During [former Ukrainian president] Mr. Yanukovych's time in office, all businesses were structured this way, especially those related to the mass media. All channels had companies abroad, absolutely all of them. Because this was an opportunity for politics not to influence you. In Kvartal 95 there was satire, everyone was putting on pressure, everyone wanted to have influence. The tax inspectors came to us, if not daily, then at least weekly, and for such things this was part of the "business structure" of Kvartal 95 Studio.

In May 2019, in response to a question from the *Ukrainska Pravda* (Ukrainian Truth) newspaper[1] about whether he considers Zelensky a cynical businessman, Kolomoisky said: "Very much so. He is someone not to be trifled with. No sentiments. If anyone is guilty, then he is guilty. No discussions, no excuses."

---

[1] The website for the paper is: https://www.pravda.com.ua/. For the English-language version of the paper, see: https://www.pravda.com.ua/eng/.

Despite these issue with finances, Zelensky and his team won much more than they may have lost at 1+1. Because it was on the 1+1 TV channel in November 2015 that the series *Servant of the People* was aired, in which the current president played the role of the high-school history teacher Vasyl Holoborodko, who would become head of state. In fact, thanks to this image, after four years a new political reality was constructed in Ukraine, in which the main role went to Volodymyr Zelensky, and the eponymous political party became the ruling party in the country.

Both Kolomoisky and Zelensky unanimously claim that when *Servant of the People* was launched on air, they never suspected that they would all end up in politics. But Ihor Valeriyovych Kolomoisky and Volodymyr Oleksandrovych Zelensky are, of course, clever. Because on December 2, 2017, the Party of Decisive Changes was renamed the Servant of the People Party.

Apparently, the business partners were going to play politics. They could hardly have imagined how this game was going to end for both of them. By that time, Kolomoisky had already been removed from his post as head of the Dnipropetrovsk ODA; his Privatbank had been nationalized; and he remained abroad. To be on the safe side. Kolomoisky, of course, had been insulted by Poroshenko. He sought revenge. More precisely, he was ready to do everything in his power to prevent Poroshenko from being re-elected president in 2019. A year before the election, in May 2018, Kolomoisky did not skimp on his compliments for Yuliya Tymoshenko, calling her the worthiest candidate for head of state. It seemed that the oligarch had already placed his bet in the big game. And Zelensky had clearly been set up in the role, at best, of a semifinalist in the race. That is to say, anybody else in the final round with Tymoshenko, just not Poroshenko.

Even as Kolomoisky was singing the praises of Tymoshenko, his confidant Andriy Bohdan was persuading Zelensky to run for president. The latter hesitated. For almost the entire summer of 2018, Zelensky made video clips and joked about his possible presidential candidacy. However, in October it was decided: the artistic director of Kvartal 95 Studio was going to run.

Indeed, for Kolomoisky, putting forward Zelensky and Tymoshenko involved virtually no risk. He knew that one of the two candidates would win. And indeed – on New Year's Eve on the 1+1 TV channel – Ukrainians were greeted not by the then president Petro Poroshenko, but by Zelensky, who announced his intention to become president of Ukraine.

Poroshenko's supporters were offended by the 1+1 channel stunt. To their mind Kolomoisky had acted in the role of the evil Karabas Barabas,[1] and Zelensky in the role of an obedient puppet. Perhaps this boosted Kolomoisky's pride, but it really annoyed Zelensky.

Were these assertions, highlighted by Poroshenko, that Zelensky was a puppet of Kolomoisky justified? This was probably political hyperbole, which was tied to the fact that Zelensky was a political novice. Ukraine had never before had a president who took on the reins of governing without any previous experience in public administration. Hence the idea of Zelensky as a puppet incapable of being president. And if there is a puppet, it means that someone has to pull the strings. The logic is absolutely clear. As well as the link to Kolomoisky. Poroshenko kept repeating: "Why are the Kremlin, its agents, fugitive oligarchs, so furiously raging in these elections? Furiously raging! They've completely lost control! We don't give Kolomoisky a chance!"

---

[1] The evil character in Aleksei Tolstoy's *The Golden Key, or the Adventures of Buratino* (1936), which is based on the Pinocchio story.

It seems that during the presidential campaign Poroshenko was aiming his fight against Kolomoisky, and not against Zelensky. And this, evidently, was a fatal mistake for which Poroshenko paid with the position of head of state.

Even before the inauguration of President Zelensky, on May 16, 2019, after two years of self-exile in Geneva and Tel Aviv, Kolomoisky returned to Ukraine. He felt really triumphant. His candidate had won the election, and he believed the world was now in his pocket. Or at least that of Privatbank.

After Zelensky won the presidential election, Kolomoisky, who had previously avoided excessive attention from journalists, gave several lengthy interviews. In particular, the Russian publication *RBK*[1] in which the Ukrainian oligarch pondered the future of the country, commented on appointments of personnel, and hinted at his close relations with the new president. It was as if Kolomoisky had been elected president and not Zelensky. He did not hide his satisfaction over the fact that he was considered a shadow president. Commenting on Zelensky's victory, Kolomoisky said: "I'm thrilled!" And why wouldn't he be thrilled? His former business partner was elected president, his personal attorney was in charge of the Office of the President, the former director of Kvartal 95, who was appearing on 1+1, became head of the SBU, some of the deputies of the Servant of the People Party were affiliated with Kolomoisky. Life, it seemed, was good.

At the start of his presidential career, Zelensky was compared with Putin, and Kolomoisky with Boris Berezovsky (a former Russian business tycoon who helped Putin rise to power). However, such analogies are schematic. For if everything were so simple and linear, Kolomoisky would

---

[1] Russian Business Consulting: https://www.rbc.ru/.

not have constantly to hint in the interview that he was "king of the beasts." For a true king sits in the shadows and calmly waits for his next victim to be brought to him. He doesn't need to remind the entire "forest" that he is the strongest, wisest, and quickest. For a person who really has power in Ukraine, such behavior seems quite strange. Not only money, but influence too likes not to be overly visible. But Kolomoisky, given his behavior, thinking, and actions, is a typical representative of the 1990s. For him, a keyring with the inscription "Zelensky," which he plays with in his fingers, is a symbol of might and omnipotence. He's working on the audience.

During the first half year of Zelensky's presidency and up to the resignation of Andriy Bohdan from the post of head of the Office of the President, rumors abounded about communications between Zelensky and Kolomoisky. They concerned recordings that Kolomoisky allegedly used to blackmail Zelensky. Others were about secret meetings between the president and the oligarch.

Kolomoisky sincerely expected that, with the ascent to power of "his" president, the question about Privatbank would be closed in his favor. Between the first and second rounds of the presidential election, in one of his interviews, the oligarch said: "I don't need Privatbank, just let them return my two billion." For a year the Zelensky team made no moves against Kolomoisky. But, at the insistence of the IMF, the Ukrainian Parliament voted for an "anti-Kolomoisky" law regarding banks, which closed Kolomoisky's path to have his ownership of Privatbank returned. This did not prevent 16,000 amendments to the act from being put forward by deputies, whom Kolomoisky controlled, or behind-the-scenes negotiations, which obviously occurred.

However, Kolomoisky was not used to losing. He was

always ready to fight. Even when it seemed that everyone was against him. Even when the FBI was investigating him for possible money-laundering in the United States, and when he was *persona non grata* in the United States.

To protect his interests, the oligarch is ready for anything. Including replacing the president. And President Zelensky should always remember this.

Zelensky shouldn't ever forget the story about Kolomoisky and the tie. Just in case.

Episode 23

Poroshenko on His Knees

If someone had said to Poroshenko a few years earlier that his main competitor in the 2019 presidential election would be a comedian, I think he would have laughed out loud, as he knows how to do.

Who? Vova Zelensky? This clown from the Kvartal? His competitor? It just couldn't be. Poroshenko would have been even more surprised if someone had said to him that he would get crushed by an actor in a vote of 73 percent to 25 percent.

The political heavyweight was ready to do battle with Yuliya Tymoshenko or Yuriy Boyko, but not with Volodymyr Zelensky. He had trodden a long path in politics, so he understood perfectly well: miracles just do not happen in Ukraine. It took him sixteen years to reach the pinnacle of the presidency. Membership in the SDPU(o) (Social Democratic Party of Ukraine (united)), participation in the creation of the Party of Regions, with Yushchenko in opposition, secretary of the RNBO, a public argument with Yuliya Tymoshenko and resignation, foreign minister in Tymoshenko's government, minister of economic development in Azarov's government, and the presidency. Poroshenko played by the rules that were at work in Ukraine. In 2019, Zelensky broke them.

By the end of 2018, Poroshenko's staff seemed convinced that Poroshenko's main competitor in the presidential campaign was Yuliya Tymoshenko. All opinion polls indicated that the Batkivshchyna (Homeland Party) leader was in competition with the incumbent president. Political strategists, of course, did suggest that a Macron-like figure could appear in Ukraine. Ukrainians' need for a new face was strong. However, hardly anyone ever imagined that Zelensky, joining the election campaign on December 31, 2018, would reach the final of the presidential election.

Although, as Roman Bezsmertny says, Poroshenko had been aware of Zelensky for a long time, and understood him:

> He figured Zelensky out much earlier and understood that he was backed by Kolomoisky. And I can say from my conversations with his very close entourage that he understood how it would turn out and knew this result long before that. And I understood certain aspects of this result. Moreover, I can say that we underestimate the analytical schools that operate in the Ukrainian governmental system. I know for certain that these schools reported to Poroshenko on the results of this election, even according to region. And he knew this. Another thing is that he, as a political fighter, couldn't afford to draw back. There were really heated conversations, beginning with the head of the Office of the President of Ukraine Borys Lozhkin, all the way to the presidential aides. And thanks to the fact that completely open-minded people participated in these conversations, all of whom, from childhood, were infected by the bacillus of democracy, such as Yuriy Lutsenko, Ihor Hryniv, and the same Borys Lozhkin, they told Poroshenko the truth. And

he knew this, he heard this, and understood it perfectly. But this political "animal nature," in the good sense of the word, this bestial instinct, did not allow him to back away.

According to Bezsmertny, the situation in which Poroshenko ended up was caused by his own policies, which consisted of browbeating everyone around him and not allowing them opportunity for growth. That is why, Bezsmertny surmises, the fifth president of Ukraine failed to succeed in nurturing a successor.

The political strategist Serhiy Haidai, who at one time worked with Poroshenko and advised the staff of the Batkivshchyna Party leader during the 2019 presidential election, reasons that Poroshenko's and Tymoshenko's staffs were preparing to win the main prize of the campaign – the presidency. And, he claimed, Poroshenko never doubted his victory. Haidai says that Poroshenko had his own vision of the voter:

He believes that a voter is a shallow person who simply forgets what he is promised from one election to another. And he wants to hear certain lies during the campaign. The elections consist of a kind of competition between liars. And people vote for the most talented and boldest one. Poroshenko played this role. He once said to me, "Well, they want to hear what they want to hear from the stage at a given time." And let tomorrow take care of itself. Yes, something is forgotten by the voters, but still a certain negative attitude is formed: he doesn't keep his promises, he is prepared to lie. And Petro Oleksiyovych [Poroshenko], I'm sorry to say, is the biggest liar of them all. We remember that in 2014 his campaign was really daring and filled with lies: "I will end the war in a day, maybe two. Each combatant will receive thousands in 'combat pay' and will be insured

for two million. I'll sell all my assets, besides channel 5."
What else did he promise? He promised that the exchange
rate for the dollar would be ten. I remember one of the
voters, somewhere near the stage, hollering at him: "Oh,
he's lying!" And Poroshenko looks at him and points with
his finger: "Here, you, write it down, it will be ten." The guy
asks, "When?" His answer: "May 26," the day of his election.
He didn't foresee that this was leading him to the edge of an
abyss. But it wasn't just this doing that; it was the situation
in general.

That is, Poroshenko has always believed that power is
given to the elected so that they can enrich themselves and
be a particular immune caste of people who know how to
use power for their own self-enrichment.

From the moment of the official registration of Volodymyr
Zelensky as a presidential candidate, Poroshenko's team
strove to persuade the Kvartal 95 Studio artistic director
to debate with him. Poroshenko is an excellent orator. He
was convinced that, in order to show his superiority over
Zelensky, he need only to have a public discussion with the
actor. For almost the entire presidential campaign Zelensky
avoided publicity, understanding perfectly that questions of
state-building and political and economic processes were
not his strong points. Already at the beginning of 2019,
political scientists did not rule out that Zelensky would be
one of the finalists in the race, and Poroshenko's staff became
more insistent about a presidential debate. In the public
arena, both Poroshenko and the pool of political strategists
who were affiliated with him began to spread the notion
that Zelensky was a puppet of Kolomoisky. Poroshenko's
team reproached the "kvartalization" of contacts with
Russia and presumed that if Zelensky were to become president it would mean a victory for the Kremlin. Billboards

even appeared on the country's highways with two photos: Poroshenko and Putin – that is to say, Ukrainians, make up your mind between Poroshenko and Zelensky. Without any alternatives. Although, according to the version of political strategist Serhiy Haidai, Poroshenko's team was preparing for the eventuality that, in the second round of the presidential election, he would still be competing against one of the leaders of the Opposition Platform Za Zhyttya! (For Life!). These billboards – Poroshenko and Putin – Haidai maintains, were the "readymade joke concoctions" of the staff of the fifth president of Ukraine.

At the same time, rumors about Zelensky's drug addiction began to spread across the media. "The hand of Moscow," "Kolomoisky's puppet," "drug addict," "clown." The more opponents pressed Zelensky, the faster his approval rating grew. And they expected Poroshenko to bring him down in a public debate. I am certain this was Poroshenko's team's main strategic mistake. Such mistakes had also been espoused by the staffs of former Ukrainian presidents Leonid Kravchuk and Viktor Yushchenko, who considered the competitors of their bosses to be incapable of discussion.

However, as it happened, after long negotiations by correspondence, on April 19, 2019, two days before the presidential election, the candidates came together in a debate at the NSK Olympic Stadium. Poroshenko's expectations were not fulfilled. Despite making several mistakes, Zelensky was well prepared for the discussion – *KVK* is *KVK*. More to the point, he managed to bring Poroshenko to his knees at the stadium. In fact, this was initiated by Zelensky himself. He was answering Poroshenko's question regarding whether he, if elected president, was ready to kneel before Putin.

Zelensky answered that the words "getting down on your knees" were taken out of context. He said:

Regarding knees, the words are ripped out from a phrase. Before the war, when our people, our Ukrainians, were already on the Maidan, there were those who had already perished, and I addressed each one of the presidents, and said to Yanukovych: "Be so kind as to step down from the post of presidency, ease your mind." Then I turned to Putin and said, "I'm ready to go down on my knees, just don't bring Ukraine to its knees."

Poroshenko shook his head in disbelief at these words.

Zelensky continued: "I am now ready to kneel before every mother who did not see her son come back from the front, before every child who did not see their father come home, before every wife who did not see her husband come home. And I invite you to do the same," and he knelt. Poroshenko also knelt down on one knee, kissing the national flag, which volunteer Tetyana Rychkova, whose husband had died in 2014 near Yenakiyeve, was holding.

The debate was a victory for Zelensky.

His phrase addressed to Poroshenko, "I am not your opponent, I am your verdict," and the slogan "When spring comes – let's start planting [crooks behind bars]," (which, according to Andriy Bohdan, he invented), largely determined the outcome of the 2019 election.

After the victory, Zelensky's team tried to move as quickly as possible into the presidential administration offices. Zelensky sincerely believed that Poroshenko and his staff were consciously delaying the process of transfer of power.

The majority of Ukrainians were convinced that Poroshenko himself, surrounded by his friends, business partners, and cronies, was to blame for all their troubles. Voters thirsted for justice and expected former officials to be sent to jail. But Zelensky's team did not satisfy this demand.

Did Zelensky really want to put Poroshenko behind bars? He surely did. Zelensky was convinced that, in becoming president, he would solve this problem really quickly. But it turned out that the desire alone of the head of state is not enough. In the end, there are laws, procedures, organs of investigation, the courts. Educated as a lawyer, Zelensky, theoretically, should have understood this.

But no. Over the course of the year, the sixth president of Ukraine demanded that the security services investigate Poroshenko and his associates, but they were in no hurry to fulfill the president's orders. As a result, in March 2020 Prosecutor General Ruslan Ryaboshapka, whom Zelensky, in a telephone conversation with Trump, had said would be "one hundred percent my man," was fired.

Ryaboshapka says that his resignation resulted from intrigues of the then acting director of the DBR, who succeeded him in the Office of the Prosecutor General. As Ryaboshapka told me:

> From the DBR certain documents were regularly received regarding cases against Petro Poroshenko, and, to put it mildly, the quality of these cases was very low. Parallel to that, there were public steps, especially concerning the fact that the DBR had prepared a draft of allegations against Poroshenko and that the DBR was preparing to imprison Poroshenko for this or that . . . At first there were public pronouncements, and only afterward did documents come to the prosecutor's office, the quality of which was very bad. That is, everyone had the impression that the DBR was working, but that the prosecutor's office was putting a stop to all these investigations. I lost my patience. I went to Zelensky and showed him a draft of allegations prepared by the DBR, which did not stand up to any criticism. There were a bunch of mistakes, even grammatical ones, not to

speak of the law. Iryna Venedyktova came to the meeting and, instead of commenting on the quality of the document prepared by them, in front of the president began to accuse me of ostensibly having certain criminal proceedings for sale. When I asked where and which ones I'm selling, she replied that I sell them at NABU. There was a complete lack of logic in what she said. She didn't name a single proceeding. A scandal erupted, and from this I drew conclusions about what she had shown to Zelensky before and what opinion he formed. Well, finally it ended with her becoming the next prosecutor general, that is, she had motives to get me fired. Additionally, we have been quite active with NABU in many cases linked to the oligarchs, including Kolomoisky in the affairs of Privatbank. These oligarchs sensed a threat and also conveyed relevant messages to the president.

Ryaboshapka says that Ruslan Stefanchuk, a close friend of Zelensky, introduced Venedyktova to the president. According to him, she was recommended as a person whom he could trust. Ryaboshapka maintains:

She has demonstrated this loyalty in every way and keeps demonstrating it to Zelensky. With regard to her level of expertise, we see that there is none at all. She had about the same level of training in the law as Zelensky. And from all sides, from all camps, accusations reverberate that, as a lawyer and as a prosecutor, she is really weak. That is, the first explanation is loyalty [to Zelensky] and friendship with Stefanchuk, and the second, perhaps, is what Bohdan indicated when he explained the principles by which people are now being appointed to Zelensky's team – the worse they are, the better.

It's surprising that, despite all Zelensky's bombastic state-ments about corruption in Poroshenko's associates, the new team failed to prove even a single case in court. This, to be honest, is frankly surprising. Especially when you consider the fact that during the presidential campaign, several journalistic investigations emerged concerning which of Poroshenko's friends are dirty. But the fact remains: over the course of three springs, Zelensky was unable to put Poroshenko behind bars as he had promised.

The Office of the Prosecutor General and the State Bureau of Investigation conducted dozens of criminal proceedings against Poroshenko, from incitement of religious hatred to treason. By then, the ex-president had been charged for accepting *tomos*,[1] for issuing orders to defend the Donbas in summer 2014, and for sending Ukrainian boats across the Kerch Strait in fall 2018. The scope of claims against Poroshenko was really wide and at times quite curious, which permitted the former president to publicly ridicule Zelensky's team. Petro Oleksiyovych addressed the president in the courtroom:

Volodymyr Oleksandrovych, my dear friend, no one fears you. Neither in this hall, nor outside. And your decrees for the imprisonment of Poroshenko are a criminal offense. In Ukraine, in Europe, and in the world. I want to repeat to you one more time: my team and I deeply love Ukraine. We honor and respect the institution of the presidency. You are not our enemy, and we need not fear you. Our enemy is Putin, whom you failed to mention in your interview.

However, the case of the appointment of Serhiy Semochko as deputy chairman of the SZR (Foreign Intelligence Service), which was heard in the Pechersk

---

[1] A decree of autocephaly granted to the Ukrainian Orthodox Church in January 2019 by Ecumenical Patriarch Bartholomew. This removed the Ukrainian Church from the jurisdiction of the Russian Orthodox Church.

District Court of Kyiv, turned out, perhaps, to be one of
the most inconsequential imaginable for the fifth president of Ukraine. In effect, it turned Poroshenko into a
dissident and a martyr of the regime, and Zelensky into a
person who persecutes his political opponents. After all,
essentially, they wanted to punish Poroshenko for sign-
ing documents to make personnel appointments, which
was within his powers. Determining the constitutionality
of these decrees is the responsibility not of the prosecutor's office, the DBR, or NABU investigators, but of the
constitutional court.

The uncertainty of prosecutors and investigators,
together with Poroshenko's and his lawyers' strong public
speaking skills, turned his trial into a political showcase.
The public failures of Zelensky and his team forced even
Poroshenko's convinced opponents to side with the ex-
president, clearly articulating their demand during the days
of the trial: "Away with Zelya!" It is in these very words
that we find the final evaluation of the dozens of criminal
proceedings that Poroshenko underwent, coming from that
active section of society that comprised not only the driving
force at the Maidan, but also set off to fight in the Donbas
in 2014.

As a result, on July 8, 2020, the Pechersk District Court of
Kyiv dismissed the motion to enact restrictive measures on
former President Poroshenko for his appointment of Serhiy
Semochko as first deputy head of the Foreign Intelligence
Service.

In January 2022, one more attempt by Zelensky's team
to send Poroshenko to jail failed. At the end of 2021, the
State Bureau of Investigation and the HPU alleged that
the fifth president of Ukraine had facilitated the activities
of a terrorist organization and had committed treason by
purchasing coal from the LPR and the DPR. Putin's crony,

Viktor Medvedchuk, was under scrutiny in the same case. The prosecutor's office insisted on taking Poroshenko into custody, but the court rejected this. A precautionary measure was enacted against Poroshenko in the form of a personal obligation that his passport be taken away so he could no longer travel abroad.

In fact, there are considerable doubts about whether Zelensky actually wants to put Poroshenko behind bars. The main task for Zelensky seems to be to keep his opponent on a short leash, showing to the voters – look, I'm keeping my promises, but investigators, prosecutors, and judges are ruining everything. For Zelensky, Poroshenko on the loose is a living embodiment of the previous illicit power. He can always be called in for questioning by the prosecutor's office or to a court hearing. Poroshenko in prison would lead to a mass street demonstration by his supporters, which might result in a new Maidan.

Poroshenko is trying to squeeze out the maximum dividends from this situation. The ex-president knows perfectly well that, with the support of leaders of Western countries, the current Ukrainian government would not dare put him in jail. That is why he acts today as the leader of all national democratic forces and as a serious counterweight to Zelensky.

As strange as it may sound today, Zelensky and Poroshenko simply just need each other. They are perfect political sparring partners. Against opponents smaller in stature, Zelensky would look really pathetic, and Poroshenko would not look as powerful and majestic. Their confrontation looks epic and large scale – as it was in 2019. The former is trying to play the role of president, the latter can't escape from his role. Zelensky and Poroshenko are simply doomed to fight against each other. At least until a new president appears in Ukraine.

Still, Roman Bezsmertny is convinced that the confrontation between Poroshenko and Zelensky is an exclusively Kremlin scenario. In his words:

> The Kremlin is constantly trying to heat up the Poroshenko–Zelensky paradigm. Otherwise, Zelensky would not periodically open such foolish criminal cases against Poroshenko. Take note: there were fifteen of them. Some have been closed, but now even more have been opened. This means that there are people around Zelensky who follow the will of the Kremlin and impose on him not only the discourse of the Kremlin, but also the paradigm.

At the beginning of the Russo-Ukrainian war, Poroshenko announced that he had reached an understanding with Zelensky. Now, he says, he and Zelensky are on the same team.

Episode 24

The Zelensky Collective

After January 15, 2020, the day of the publication of the audio recording in which then Prime Minister Oleksiy Honcharuk made comments about Zelensky's poor command of economics, it became obvious that he had only a few days left as the head of government.

The guys, naturally, shook hands for the TV cameras. Zelensky gave Honcharuk one more chance. The prime minister, with the look of a guilty schoolboy caught in the act, accepted it. It looked as if the misunderstanding between Zelensky and Honcharuk was now in the past. However, despite public statements from both about peace, friendship, and "chewing gum,"[1] the political tandem was finished.

Observers began to notice a high level of distrust in Honcharuk's government. More than 50 percent of Ukrainians failed to support the activities of the cabinet of ministers. Understandably, this affected Zelensky's

---

[1] This is the literal translation of the Russian expression that might be rendered in English by a dynamically equivalent expression such as "peace, love, and harmony."

popularity ratings. The president needed to channel the negativity that was growing among the people. Honcharuk's team, certainly, made many mistakes, including the awarding of bonuses to his team of three times the amount of their salaries, a failure to communicate with Ukrainians about the protests at Novi Sanzhary,[1] budget shortfalls, and overseeing a decline in industrial production. The failures of Honcharuk's team, combined with Zelensky's obvious weakness, would inevitably lead to the failure of ZeKomanda (the Zelensky team). Everyone understood that. There was only one thing to be done – the government should voluntarily resign.

On March 4, the Verkhovna Rada accepted the resignation of Honcharuk's government. Honcharuk did not provide clear explanations as to why he resigned from his position prematurely. Two days earlier, he said that he had no intention of leaving. And during his farewell speech in the Rada, he talked a lot about his achievements and about the fact that he did not resort to stealing.

On the same day, President Zelensky addressed many kind words to both Honcharuk and his team. He said that they had done a good job, but, unfortunately, that was not enough. We need technocrats, time to realize reforms, we need to conquer new heights. Honcharuk was replaced by Denys Shmygal, who had spent a month in the previous government as deputy prime minister and minister of development of communities and territories. Prior to that, he was head of the Ivano-Frankivsk ODA, and before that he worked in the commercial structures of the oligarch Rinat Akhmetov. Zelensky was confident that the newly elected prime minister and the fifteen ministers appointed on

---

[1] On February 20, 2020, protesters blocked buses of COVID Ukrainian evacuees from China coming into the town of Novi Sanzhary in the Poltava Region to be quarantined.

March 4 would be able to restore the people's confidence in his team. It is difficult to say on what such optimism was based. Because Shmygal's team turned out to be a group of fellow travelers in a single government train carriage, who could be pushed from it at the first bidding of the train's conductor, Volodymyr Zelensky.

The haste with which Shmygal's government was formed meant that some key posts remained vacant, namely the ministers of economy, education, culture, energy, and the coal industry, which, when it came to voting in the Verkhovna Rada, was all too evident. Those who were offered posts right up to the last minute refused to become part of Shmygal's team. The then minister of internal affairs Arsen Avakov retained his seat – this was the fifth government he had served in six years. The minister of justice Denys Malyuska, the minister of infrastructure Vladyslav Krykliy, and the minister of digital transformation Mykhailo Fedorov also stayed in place. Dmytro Kuleba and Vadym Prystaiko exchanged posts, the former becoming minister of foreign affairs and the latter deputy prime minister for European integration. All the other new appointments consisted of people who had already been in power under former presidents Kuchma, Yushchenko, and Yanukovych, and who had ties to domestic oligarchs.

During his appointment hearings, Shmygal behaved like a student sitting an exam, limiting himself to general phrases. Understandably, given the experience of his predecessor, Shmygal tried to choose his words wisely. They turned out to be shallow and not very convincing. Among those who entered government with him were those who agreed to risk their reputations, and those who had lost them long ago.

Later on, numerous attempts by Shmygal to approve the government's plan of action in the Verkhovna Rada, where the president's Servant of the People Party had a majority, were unsuccessful. The prime minister's ill-advised public statements about the possibility of supplying water from Ukraine to occupied Crimea, his promises to create 500,000 jobs in May 2021 for those who lost their jobs during the coronavirus crisis, and attempts to stop labor migration for the same reason – Shmygal's government turned out to be openly weak and incapable of working in the conditions created by the pandemic.

The opposition can endlessly discuss the weakness of the ZeKomanda staff. However, practically speaking, almost all power in Ukraine belongs to Volodymyr Zelensky. It was he, not the parliamentary majority, who decided the fate of Honcharuk's government. It was he, not the Verkhovna Rada, who determined who would be a minister – in Parliament there was no discussion whatsoever about potential candidates for the ministerial posts. And it was the president himself, not the prime minister or the speaker of Parliament, who would be responsible for the actions of the entire team. Therefore, no matter whose name is entered in the column under "prime minister" or "minister," it might just as well be "Zelensky."

However, having the trust of the Ukrainian people is also a great responsibility. Not just for the voters themselves, but also for the sake of the future of the state.

Incidentally, political strategist Serhiy Haidai in 2020 did not believe that Zelensky was capable of changing himself or those in his circle. "If he didn't just change as a result of the challenges he faced in his first year, and the system tamed him, I don't believe he will change in the future," he said.

And the people's deputy of Ukraine, Geo Leros, who publicly accused Zelensky and his circle of corruption and bribery, is more explicit:

Zelensky is not ready for criticism. He holds a position that doesn't correspond to his scale of state thinking. When I began to criticize his closest inner circle, I became a traitor. Because, to his mind, if there are facts of corruption, a team player should remain silent about it. This is Zelensky's thinking. And he managed to do the same regarding other people. I think Zelensky should resign from the office of president. A complete reboot of the president, the Verkhovna Rada, and the cabinet of ministers is needed. If he wants, let him come out to the people with a new program. Because he did not keep his promises.

This was the case until February 2022. What will happen after the end of the Russo-Ukrainian war no one knows. Not even Zelensky himself.

Episode 25
Zelensky's Idol Syvokho

In 1989, a new TV star appeared in the *KVK* Premier League in Moscow – Serhiy Syvokho, a member of the Donetsk Polytechnic Institute (DPI) team. He was 20 years old at the time. He was quick-witted and had a good voice. When Syvokho turned up on the stage of the Club of the Cheerful and Quick-Witted, musical parodies began to surface of contemporary Soviet pop music idols: Sergei Krylov, Vladimir Presnyakov the younger, Sergei Chelobanov, and Mikhail Shufutinsky. Syvokho really stood out, not only on the DPI team, but also on the Soviet national stage in general.

Syvokho's team reached the *KVK* finals twice, but never won the Premier League. In 1993, the DPI team merged with the Ural Polytechnic Institute team and became known as the Dream Team, which became a semi-finalist in the league, but never won.

At the time when Serhiy Anatoliyovych was conquering Soviet television, his audience included an 11-year-old boy from Kryvyi Rih, Volodya Zelensky. Apparently, this was when Syvokho, recognized as the best showman of the

Ostankino TV station, became an idol for the young actor. I am certain that hundreds and even thousands of youngsters who played schoolchildren's *KVK* at that time dreamt of being like Syvokho.

A few years would pass before Zelensky would actually meet Syvokho. From the start, both were part of the formation of the *KVK* Ukrainian League, and, after that, Kvartal 95 Studio, programs on the Inter TV channel, and, later, *The League of Laughter*. Syvokho took part in Viktor Yanukovych's 2010 presidential election campaign. "Unfortunately, I was wrong about him," Syvokho declared.

Be that as it may, Syvokho and Zelensky went shoulder to shoulder until the 2019 presidential election. Syvokho worked as a creative producer of Kvartal 95 LLC and was a co-owner and producer of Mega-Radio. With Zelensky's victory, Syvokho entered into politics himself. But he wasn't successful.

In July 2019, in the early parliamentary elections, Syvokho ran for office as a people's deputy for the Servant of the People Party in the Donbas (Election District 49). However, he was not elected. Still, Syvokho accompanied his friend the president on almost all his trips to eastern Ukraine. Syvokho strove to convince everyone that quite reasonable people live "on the other side," people whom one can engage in dialogue. Just who it was that Zelensky's old friend had in mind is not clear for sure. It's possible he meant Ismail Abdullayev, a former member of the KVK Donetsk Polytechnic Institute team, who became director of the Oplot TV regional TV channel after the establishment of the DPR. Or maybe he meant someone else whom he knew personally and with whom he maintains contact.

In October 2019, Zelensky's team designated Serhiy Syvokho ad hoc advisor to the secretary of the RNBO on reintegration and reconstruction of the Donbas. The former showman, as an erstwhile resident of Donetsk, had no doubts that his knowledge, competence, and contacts were sufficient to organize a peaceful dialogue with the occupied Donbas. However, Syvokho's first steps and statements in his new post elicited a wave of anger among the veterans of the Russo-Ukrainian war and representatives of the national democratic camp.

The position of Zelensky's friend and advisor to the RNBO, whose development had been molded in particular in Moscow, was and remains unchanged: the war in the Donbas is an internal conflict in Ukraine and can be overcome only by means of a dialogue between the two sides.

In Kyiv on March 12, 2020, Syvokho decided to create a National Platform for Reconciliation and Unity. After a brief event, journalists and ATO (Anti-Terrorist Operation) veterans surrounded him demanding that he answer the question of who started the war in the Donbas. Serhiy replied: "As you know, we have a war going on, a hybrid war. One method of waging war is to initiate an internal conflict and then get support for it from the Russian Federation."

Those surrounding Syvokho were dissatisfied with his words. Someone shouted from the crowd, "You hybrid idiot!" Syvokho understood that he needed to retreat because he might otherwise get into a fistfight. He tried to break his way out of the circle, at which point he fell over. After getting up, he quickly left the room where the inauguration of the National Platform for Reconciliation and Unity was taking place.

To quell public outrage, the RNBO secretary Oleksiy Danilov had to announce that one of the eleven ad hoc advisors, Serhiy Syvokho, was not authorized to represent the council. After a short period of time, the "credentials" of this freelance advisor to the RNBO were removed from the former *KVK* member. However, despite this, Syvokho stated that Zelensky had sufficient strength and abilities to make sweeping decisions. "I knew Zelensky even before his presidency. Even then he knew how to engage in wide-ranging actions. But a very heavy burden of responsibility lies on him."

It is noteworthy that during the entire time that Syvokho was absorbing all the "rays of hate," Zelensky did not say a word about his friend's so-called peace initiatives. Perhaps this is because childhood idols are like plush little teddy bears – cherished, beloved, even when they are completely faded and with one ear completely torn off.

Episode 26

The Polygraph for "Servants of the People"

Throughout the presidential campaign, Volodymyr Zelensky never tired of reiterating that there would be no room on his team for corrupt officials, schemers, or other dirty-handed bureaucrats. And if there are in the noble "herd" any bad sheep, they'll find themselves in jail. "The law will be one for all," Zelensky promised.

However, after a few months the "servants of the people" whom Zelensky brought to the Verkhovna Rada found themselves embroiled in their first corruption scandal. On October 23, 2019, the SAP (Anti-Corruption Prosecutor's Office) opened a criminal case involving fourteen people's deputies, eleven of whom were members of the Servant of the People Party. They were alleged to have received $30,000 each for voting at a meeting of a Verkhovna Rada committee against a bill to eliminate corruption schemes in real estate valuations. As a result, the bill did not pass.

Back in August, Davyd Arakhamiya, leader of the Servant of the People Party, had promised that Zelensky's team would create a "Big Brother" system that would monitor the voting of deputies from the presidential faction. Indeed, thanks to special algorithms it would be possible to eliminate all chance of corruption. But it turned out that no system would be necessary for such a battle: there would be sufficient suspicion and leaking of information in the mass media.

The bill regarding the appraisal of real estate, for the failure of which eleven members of the Servant of the People Party were blamed, called for the elimination of a corrupt system allegedly created by people's deputy Anton Yatsenko. At least that's what the authors of the bill said about the document, which members of the parliamentary committee on finance, tax, and customs policy voted for. In turn, one of those accused of bribery, Oleksandr Dubinsky, asserted that real estate appraisers had lobbied for the failed document and backed the substitution of one corruption scheme for another. In precisely this way, Dubinsky explains his hesitancy in voting for the bill.

The Office of the President of Ukraine proposed to resolve the conflict with the help of a polygraph. But without the participation of NABU detectives, SAP, or HPU employees. Davyd Arakhamiya even promised to present a witness on TV who was present at the time the bribe was offered. However, a public accusation of bribery was sufficient on its own for an investigation to be opened by anti-corruption organs. Even more so because there was a witness.

As it happened, all these "maneuvers" ended up with a fake polygraph test, which Davyd Arakhamiya and Oleksandr Dubinsky took in turn on live TV. Both got away with it.

In large measure, the "servants of the people" could themselves resolve their internal conflicts. Without polygraphs, SAP, or the Office of the President. But it didn't work out that way. The presidential faction consists of an exceedingly diverse membership. Some said Ihor Kolomoisky was to blame for his influence on the Servant of the People Party, others said the newly elected deputies fell victim to their own greed, while others said the party that consisted of 254 deputies would, sooner or later, be doomed to become a political *Titanic*.

In the end, President Zelensky was forced to intervene in the scandal in the party, where accusations of corruption were circulating. During a visit to Japan, he proposed, via a post on his Facebook page, that all members, without exception, of the parliamentary committee on finance, tax, and customs policy (the majority of whom are representatives of the Servant of the People Party) should submit to a polygraph test. In the words of the president: "If it is established that there is even the slightest possibility that one of the deputies took money for their vote in the committee . . . anti-corruption organs" will deal with them. That is to say, no mercy would be shown to anyone: neither to their people nor to others. The only question, actually, was just who Zelensky considered to be his people and who the others.

One of Zelensky's slogans, which he used during the election campaign, went like this: "When spring comes – let's start planting [crooks behind bars]." The presidential candidate promised Ukrainians that corrupt officials who were in power under Petro Poroshenko would be "planted [in jail]." But only a handful ended up behind bars. By November 1, 2019, Zelensky was anticipating reports from law-enforcement agencies on decisive actions regarding allegations of high-profile corruption. But instead of this, his own associates were suspected of corruption.

The story of the accusations against the eleven deputies from the Servant of the People Party fizzled away to nothing. None of the suspects ended up in jail, not a single one of them resigned their post as a people's deputy.

Another month would pass, and the former people's deputy from the Servant of the People Party, Anna

Skorokhod, declared that, among the president's faction, deputies were receiving additional payments of $5,000. All the "servants," without exception, especially the then head of the Verkhovna Rada Dmytro Razumkov, categorically repudiated these allegations. Nevertheless, rumors began to circulate through the lobbies about top-up payments to party leaders, which seemed to be several times higher than the parliamentary top-up payments.

The president can swear as much as he wants that his intentions are crystal clear and can call for a fight against corruption, but if there is someone in his team whose hands are dirty, presidential statements will be worthless. Even if all the "former government officials" end up behind bars.

Episode 27

Who Turned Zelensky into an Addict?

On February 8, 2019, Zelensky arrived in Lviv as a presidential candidate. A charity performance of Kvartal 95 was planned there. At the entrance to the local arena, where the event was supposed to take place, ATO veterans (from the war in eastern Ukraine) and members of patriotic organizations met Zelensky and his team. They encircled Zelensky and publicly demanded that he not run for president. One of Zelensky's opponents uttered: "Vova, pass the drug tests. If you're clean – there's nothing to be afraid of."

In fact, it was from this very moment that the public began discussing whether Zelensky really was a drug addict. Memes, jokes on social networks, a video in which Zelensky is behaving badly, rumors spreading that, even during his acting days, the police had turned up at the Zelensky home, in response to a call, to try to get him to regain consciousness, etc. All these "dark" rumors were spread among the public, and reiterated by political strategists.

After the first round of the presidential election, on March 31, Zelensky went to the briefing in a rather unusual state.

He spoke more slowly, and his behavior was distinctive from what we had observed during the election campaign. "He's an addict!" started to appear again on Facebook.

Realizing that he could not avoid these accusations before the second round of elections, on April 3, Zelensky published his first appeal to Petro Poroshenko demanding that he undergo a drug test. Inviting his opponent to a debate at the Olympic National Sports Complex, Zelensky said: "The candidates need to pass a medical examination and prove to the people that there are no alcoholics or drug addicts among them. The country needs a healthy president." Zelensky felt that if he refused a medical examination, which, by the way, is not mandatory for presidential candidates, he would lose the support of some of his constituents before the end of the presidential campaign.

Poroshenko's staff accepted Zelensky's challenge. On April 5, Poroshenko invited Zelensky to the Olympic NSK Medical Center. However, he didn't show up. Poroshenko had blood taken for testing at four different clinics. Zelensky went to a private Eurolab clinic owned by his longtime friend Andriy Palchevsky. Vladyslav Kiryakulov, a masseur and former participant of the Ukrainian culinary show *Master Chef*, and actor in the *In-laws* TV series, took his blood. This made the situation even more absurd.

Poroshenko's team accused Zelensky of attempting to avoid independent testing for alcohol and drugs. Additionally, there was an inaccuracy that instilled doubts in Zelensky's opponents about the validity of the Eurolab tests, which were negative for both drugs and alcohol. Zelensky's Facebook page published data from April 2, 2019, although he passed the tests on April 5. The mistake, of course, was corrected by referring to the fact that they just mixed up the files in the private clinic. However, there remained a sense that someone was trying to falsify his test results.

Poroshenko's staff and media resources associated with the fifth president continued to "pound out" the theme of Zelensky's drug addiction.

On April 11, Denys Manzhosov, a childhood friend of Zelensky and ex-participant of Kvartal 95 Studio, appeared on TV. He announced a press conference in Kyiv that day. No one could find out what Zelensky's old friend wanted to say. Instead, he went on air with Matviy Hanapolsky, who asked him if he had ever witnessed Zelensky allegedly using drugs. Zelensky's old friend categorically denied it, emphasizing that it was "nonsense sucked out of thin air." The interviewer seemed to be expecting another answer. And so, for the second time he came in with the question: "Have you never seen him smoke, jab himself, etc. – so you think that's not true?" Manzhosov repeated: "It's not true." This, in fact, put this "scandal" to bed.

However, despite this, the slogan "Zelensky is a drug addict" continued to live a life of its own. Poroshenko repeated it incessantly on various TV channels between the first and second rounds: "I do not claim that Volodymyr Zelensky is a drug addict. I have no reason to believe it. I emphasize the right of Ukrainian citizens to have 100 percent guarantees that the future PRESIDENT and supreme commander-in-chief is guaranteed free from drug addiction."

But the more that Poroshenko repeated "Zelensky is not a drug addict," the more Ukrainians and his main opponent would hear the words: "drug addict, drug addict."

On April 12, 2019, Zelensky's mother, Rimma, told Hromadske TV that her son had been called a drug addict mistakenly. "He doesn't smoke cigarettes, he doesn't take anything," she said.

A few days later, in an online interview with *Apostrophe* magazine [https://apostrophe.ua], Olena Zelensky explained how she reacted to the numerous accusations about her husband's purported drug addiction:

> When there is no such thing and there never was, it's all very tiresome. Not only we, our friends too, are tired of this, as are those who were silent about it at first, although we are not trying to influence anyone. We are not asking singers and artists who have known us for many years to support us. But sometimes they themselves cannot stand this lie. They say how things really are, and that's nice. In this situation, it is sad for parents who are beginning to worry about it.

If anyone had hoped that with Zelensky's victory the topic of his drug addiction would disappear, they turned out to be wrong.

On July 6, 2020, the pro-Russian propagandist Anatoliy Shariy reported on his Telegram page that his colleagues had managed to conduct an entire special operation aimed at collecting urine from Volodymyr Zelensky at the Ryba Restaurant in Odesa. Moreover, the leader of the party named after himself claims that he ordered the analysis of the collected material for drugs in two laboratories – one Ukrainian and the other German. They say that it was with these results that Shariy allegedly tried to blackmail Zelensky's team. The pro-Kremlin blogger put a lot of effort on his YouTube channel into making Ukrainians doubt the president. At the beginning of the war, Shariy's channel was blocked in Ukraine.

On February 25, 2022, the second day of the Russo-Ukrainian war, Putin, speaking at an operational meeting of the Russian Security Council, called the leadership of Ukraine a "gang of drug addicts and neo-Nazis." In this way, the Russian president decided to support the myth of the "drug addict" Zelensky – to justify his war against Ukraine.

I expect that after Putin said "Zelensky is a drug addict," any discussion of Zelensky's drug addiction in Ukraine came to a full stop once and for all.

Episode 28

Zelensky under Yermak

During President Leonid Kuchma's first term, there were jokes in the corridors of power that he actually worked in the administration of "President" Dmytro Tabachnyk. The essence of the joke was emphasized by the influence of the head of the Office of the President and his efforts to manage everything and everyone.

The same could be said about Volodymyr Zelensky. He works in the administration of the head of the Office of the President Andriy Yermak, his old friend and a man who feels, if not like the president, then at least like the vice-president of Ukraine.

Yermak and Zelensky met when Zelensky was in charge of the Inter TV channel. Yermak's international law firm provided intellectual property and copyright protection services. Clients included Inter Media Group, Disney, Pixar, and Universal. Yermak graduated from the Kyiv Institute of International Relations (KIMV) of Taras Shevchenko Kyiv State University in 1995 and earned a master's degree in international private law. At that time, the well-known politicians Mikheil Saakashvili, Vasyl Horbal, Vitaliy Bala, and the future fifth president of Ukraine Petro Poroshenko were all enrolled at this prestigious university. KIMV constituted a veritable workshop for forging the new Ukrainian political elite.

Yermak avoided extensive political activity until 2019. For eight-and-a-half years, from May 2006 to November 2014, he was a voluntary assistant to Elbrus Tadeev, a people's deputy from the Party of Regions. However, this status and the ID of an assistant were clearly necessary for Yermak to feel at ease among the celestials on the Pechersk Hills, the seat of government. He was involved in legal support for various companies, and later began to produce films. *Squat32*, *The Rule of Battle*, and *Border* – these are the movies to which Yermak lent a hand. But he didn't achieve significant success in cinema's, especially at home. For example, while the Ukrainian-Slovak film *Border* earned $2 million abroad, in Ukraine it earned just $46,000.

All the same, despite modest experience in the movie business, his acquaintance with Volodymyr Zelensky became decisive for Yermak's future. Ten years earlier, he could hardly have imagined how this friendship with the artistic director of Kvartal 95 Studio would end. However, it is clear that the stars aligned in a way that allowed old friends to become partners in bigtime politics.

On May 21, 2019, Yermak was appointed assistant to President Zelensky. At that time, another Andriy – Bohdan – was playing a leading role in the circle of the newly elected head of state. He was also a lawyer by profession and a man who believed that he alone had made Zelensky president. Against the background of Bohdan as an expressive jokester, Yermak looked like a calm and perhaps even a somewhat phlegmatic bureaucrat. At least until becoming head of the Office of the President, he clearly knew his place and behaved himself. Perhaps that is why after only about six months Yermak became Zelensky's constant assistant in negotiations with Moscow – both on prisoner exchanges and in the preparation of the Normandy Summit in Paris. The political courage that Andriy Bohdan always publicly demonstrated was replaced by the politics of back-stage games – one of the creators of which was Andriy Yermak. The former representative in the TCG in Minsk from Ukraine, Roman Bezsmertny, asserts that the current head of the Office of the President is closely integrated into the Russian establishment and communicates with many in the presidential administration of Vladimir Putin's Russian Federation, including Dmitry Kozak and Vladislav Surkov.

At the same time, journalists on the *Schemes* program discovered that Yermak's partner in Ukrainian business was the Russian businessman Rakhamim Emanuilov. They are business partners in CJSC (Closed Joint-Stock Company) Interpromfinance Ukraine, which engages in commercial consulting, and MEP Engineering LLC. In turn, Emanuilov is a co-owner of Interpromtorg. This company is the founder of Interprombank, whose largest stockholder is a member of the Federation Council of the Federal Assembly of the Russian Federation of the Kamchatka Territory, Valery Ponomarev. Among the shareholders of the aforementioned Russian bank is Ivan Sadchikov, who is said to be the son-in-law of Sergei Prikhodko, the first deputy chief of staff in the government of the Russian Federation.

Through the stockholders of Interprombank, Yermak is also associated with Vladimir Putin's classmates – Ilgam Ragimov and Nikolai Yegorov.

Yermak says that Emanuilov is his father's old friend. They met when his father worked at the Soviet Embassy in Afghanistan. And, in the words of Yermak, he simply helped Emanuilov register a company in Ukraine. Nothing more. That is to say, no need to look for a skeleton in the closet. Nevertheless, these explanations do not give answers to the main question – how did an ordinary lawyer, Andriy Yermak, become the chief negotiator with Moscow? How did he earn the trust of Vladimir Putin's circle?

In the fall of 2019, Yermak ended up in his first serious scandal. The US Congress released details of conversations between him and the president's advisor, futurologist Ihor Novikov. At a meeting on September 14 with former state department special representative Kurt Walker and US chargé d'affaires ad interim William Taylor, Yermak and Novikov accused former President Poroshenko of killing and wounding their brothers in the east. Taylor then declared that both of them had shown photos of their relatives on their cellphones. As it turned out, thank God, both brothers turned out to be still alive. Yermak, of course, refuted this information and called it biased. However, as the saying goes, he was deemed guilty even after being proven innocent.

Later, in spring 2020, Denys, brother of the then head of the Office of the President Andriy Yermak, was involved in a corruption scandal. The people's deputy from the Servant of the People Party Geo Leros revealed video recordings in which a man who looked like the brother of the head of the Office of the President was promising his interlocutors that he would resolve the issue of employment in organs of government. But of course, not for free. The videos indicated the dates and times of recording – August 20, September 16 and 23, and October 3, 2019. In the recorded conversations, sums, positions, and means of solving "problems" are mentioned. Kyiv customs, the ministry of infrastructure, the Ukrzaliznytsia (Ukrainian Railway Company) and many other structures where the younger Yermak was ready to facilitate an appointment. Of course, this would be thanks to his brother. "My brother will come in a minute, I'll go to [his] Bankova [Street government office], and we'll discuss everything," Denys says.

The SAP, the NABU, and the DBR began to investigate Denys Yermak's case. Andriy was forced to confirm that the video recording was indeed of his brother Denys. He also indicated that he was a free citizen and not an official of the government, so he therefore had the right to talk to anyone and anywhere as head of the Ukrainian Bureau of National Development. On March 30, the DBR opened up a case against Leros for publishing the video recording of the brother of the head of the Office of the President of Ukraine. On April 23, the SAP reclassified the younger Yermak's case from "influence peddling" to "fraud" and turned it over to the national police.

The corruption scandal regarding Andriy Yermak's brother did not lead to his resignation as head of the Office of the President. He vowed to create problems for Geo Leros and he tried to find out who had recorded his brother. Interestingly, there was no immediate reaction to this scandal from President Zelensky, who, even during the election campaign, had promised to fight intensely against corruption among his staff. Only two months later, in an interview with the *Ukrainska Pravda* newspaper, did Zelensky call Denys Yermak a "chatterbox":

> And the way they dragged him in . . . He's just a chatterbox. I think a chatterbox. I consider this wrong; this is his big mistake. He always wanted to help somehow. He is like this, you know, the war – he rushed to the ATO, fought there, helped, he was a volunteer there. There is something wrong with Ukrzaliznytsia – let's find normal people. Well, he is just that kind of a person.

Zelensky added that he considers Geo Leros to be a "con artist."

But what could Zelensky say about Denys Yermak? He couldn't help but admit the guilt of the younger brother of the head of the Office of the President. Because otherwise it would turn out that both the elder Yermak and Zelensky himself were covering up for this "chatterbox," as the president expressed it.

On August 28, 2020, at about 10 p.m., unknown individuals set fire to Geo Leros's car. "My car was set on fire, this is crap," the people's deputy wrote. And two days later, President Zelensky, speaking at a congress of the Servant of the People Party, said that certain deputies from his political faction had forgotten why they had entered the Verkhovna Rada, calling them "microbes" and "bacteria." "I am sure we won't notice them on the path to success, and history will not mention their names," Zelensky said.

The next speaker at the rostrum of the Verkhovna Rada, Geo Leros, accused Zelensky of covering up corruption. The head of the SBU Ivan Bakanov, in the words of the deputy, controlled contraband, the illegal smuggling of alcohol, drug-trafficking, and trade with the ORDLO.

"Mr. President, you did not battle against the old system, you just went along with it. It was you who, with your microbes and bacteria of lies, infected the whole country, wasting the opportunity of a great state, exchanging it for envelopes from an oligarch," Leros said. Within a day he had been expelled from the Servant of the People Party, and several days later ended up being interrogated in the DBR for alleged tax evasion. Meanwhile, Zelensky called Geo a bribe-taker and a traitor.

The Office of the President has hinted multiple times at the fact that all the attacks by Geo Leros were the doing of the former head of the office, Andriy Bohdan. Still, Bohdan denies his involvement in the release of the recordings of Yermak's brother's conversations. And Leros declares that Bohdan has had nothing to do with any of his activities.

As Leros told me:

> The reason the president called me a "con artist" was because of my criticism of Andriy Yermak's actions in attempting to settle the war in eastern Ukraine. This happened after he endorsed a document on the establishment of an advisory council consisting of three TCGs in Minsk, which should include representatives of the ORDLO. Following public outrage at these actions, Zelensky's team retreated. However, I was then fired from the post of advisor to the president.

He says that his public reputation forced him to go against his own team. In the words of Geo, he did not join the people's deputies in order to chase after his mercantile interests: "I was not planning to dig for gold. I came to do something and get results."

Leros refuses to say where he acquired the recordings of Yermak's brother's conversations. According to him, two individuals are involved in the case. "It is possible that someone was conducting secret investigations in the framework of some criminal case, which was later destroyed. I doubt that it's like this – that just like this, two people with special equipment can record the brother of the then assistant to the president." Leros says that there were hints from the Office of the President "to settle this situation to mutual satisfaction," but he categorically refused. He said:

> I published materials with recordings, I published information about the so-called "VAT *skrutky*" [tax evasion

schemes]. I published material about how the "inspector" from Yermak eviscerated the capital city. No one was fired, no one was sent to jail. I waited six months for the president to put someone in jail. Instead of that, criminal proceedings have been opened against me to suppress me politically. Do you need any other evidence to prove that President Zelensky is responsible for what is happening in Ukraine? When President Zelensky calls me a traitor and a bribe-taker, he provides no evidence. When I say that his associates are corrupt and carry responsibility, I provide concrete proof.

However, let's return to the rise of Andriy Yermak's career under Volodymyr Zelensky. In fall 2019, he continued to gain political weight in the presidential circle, squeezing Andriy Bohdan out into a secondary role. Yermak became more and more indispensable to Zelensky, whether in negotiations with Moscow, or in the organization of the personal life of the president, or in foreign travel.

Zelensky's trip to Oman put an end to the story of the clash between Yermak and Bohdan over access to the "person" of the president. On January 5, 2020, Zelensky was seen on the shores of the Indian Ocean. In Ukraine, no one knew diddly-squat about the departure of the head of state, so the publication of his photo from Oman elicited surprise from the public. However, this did not last long, because the Office of the President was forced to admit that Zelensky was in Oman for meetings at the highest level. As proof of this, a photo was published of the president of Ukraine with the executive president of the State General Reserve Fund of the Sultanate of Oman, Abdulsalam al-Murshidi, and the minister responsible for foreign affairs of the Sultanate of Oman, Yusuf bin Alawi bin Abdullah. Andriy Yermak was next to him in the photo. The presence of the former was to remove doubts: Zelensky was not only on vacation; he was also working in Oman.

After Zelensky's dramatic return to Ukraine following the downing by the Iranians of an airplane owned by MAU (Ukrainian International Airlines), more than ten versions appeared about whom Zelensky had actually met in Oman. One of the main versions suggested that he met with representatives of Russia, who, they say, very masterfully "leaked" to the Internet a photo of Zelensky in a T-shirt, slippers, and baseball cap. But whatever happened, we need to remember that Zelensky was accompanied in Oman by Andriy Yermak, although, as Zelensky later admitted, his wife Olena paid for the trip. So, we need to understand that it was a family vacation.

The fate of Andriy Bohdan was actually decided after Oman. On February 11, 2020, he resigned and was replaced by Andriy Yermak, who would start almost right away positioning himself as the second person in charge in the country after Zelensky. The press service of the Office of the President began to relate information about the visits and negotiations in which Yermak gives sage advice to the head of state and others.

In August 2020, the journalist Yuriy Butusov named Andriy Yermak as being among those officials who might have participated in breaking up a special operation against the "Wagnerite" Russian mercenaries. According to the journalist, in Belarus on July 29, thirty-three members of the Wagner PVK (Private Military Company) were supposed to end up in Ukraine and stand trial for crimes committed in the Donbas. However, he says, the special operation was aborted because it had to be postponed in order not to start a quarrel with the Kremlin on the eve of the announcement of another truce in the east. For an entire year, Zelensky's team denied the very idea of conducting such a special operation.

However, later, when a group of Bellingcat journalists announced that they were investigating the circumstances surrounding the abortion of the special operation, the Office of the President of Ukraine was forced to admit that the domestic special services were indeed preparing to arrest the Wagnerites. But the special action, according to Zelensky himself, had been postponed.

On November 17, 2021, Bellingcat made public its Wagnergate report. There was no evidence that directly pointed to the fact that it was Yermak who leaked the information to the Russians about the special operation. Whatever happened, the head of the ministry of defense's main intelligence directorate, Vasyl Burba, insists that a Russian mole is sitting in the Office of the President, who has constantly and consciously disrupted special operations by Ukrainian security forces. We will obviously hear the name of this person after Ukraine's victory over Russia. If, of course, such a "mole" does exist.

Episode 29

Zelensky's Dream Team

On April 12, 2019, Emmanuel Macron was waiting for Volodymyr Zelensky and Petro Poroshenko in Paris.

Between the first and second rounds of the presidential election in Ukraine, the leader of France desired to see both candidates. It is understandable that Poroshenko had long been an acquaintance of Macron both in the negotiations in the Normandy Format and in bilateral contacts. If receiving the leader of Ukraine seemed entirely natural – as a meeting between two presidents – the appearance in the Élysée Palace of the novice politician Volodymyr Zelensky looked like a challenge to the system. The actor met with the president of France.

The finalists in the Ukrainian presidential election race flew to Paris in different ways. Zelensky was on a regular flight, on which he happily took selfies with other passengers, who then shared them on social media. Poroshenko was flown to France on the Ukrainian government's Air Force One plane. Poroshenko, of course, was met in Paris on his earlier visit as sitting president – with the participation of the Republican Guard. Zelensky was met much more simply and more informally.

Zelensky was visibly nervous during the meeting with Macron. His gestures, movements, and facial expressions betrayed the fact that he was a political novice, who until then knew about Macron only from gossip columns. It was during this meeting with the French president that Zelensky revealed his team for the first time – Ruslan Ryaboshapka, Oleksandr Danyliuk, and Ivan Bakanov. It was this trio, and his wife Olena, who accompanied Zelensky to Paris and helped him begin to understand the various nuances of international etiquette. As Ruslan Ryaboshapka recalled:

In the organization of the visit, the initiative belonged more to Danyliuk, but we joined later. It seemed that the French side also had an interest in this meeting, as the French president demonstrated clear leadership, strove to be dominant on the European continent, and it was clear that Ukraine was one of the principal countries with which France should support cooperation. That is why this meeting became possible. And the corresponding preparation lay on our shoulders as well as Danyliuk's. The delineation of the format, the delineation of the topics, what we could discuss with the French president, as well as preparing topics for Zelensky to discuss, and preparing Zelensky himself for this meeting – all this was our job. The preparation was good on both sides. Both Zelensky and Macron understood each other almost instantaneously. The foci that we chose for Zelensky were correct and found resonance with Macron. The feeling after the meeting was positive and uplifting. There was the impression that we could successfully build cooperation with France.

Macron and Zelensky are about the same age, and their

moment of appearance in politics was somewhat similar. But the similarities ended somewhere there.

The "first appraisal" (of Zelensky) in Paris was successful. After they left the Élysée Palace, one of the guards photographed the joyous four together. On his Facebook page, Zelensky signed the photo very laconically – "Dream Team." At that moment, it seemed that their friendship would never end. Zelensky's team had great political prospects. Ukraine was waiting for its own Macron.

Nine days after his trip to Paris, Zelensky was elected president of Ukraine. After he took his oath of office, his childhood friend from Kryvyi Rih, Ivan Bakanov, became head of the SBU. Ruslan Ryaboshapka was first appointed deputy head of the Office of the President and later became prosecutor general. Oleksandr Danyliuk would become secretary of the RNBO.

However, even during these early turbulent days, when the "servants of the people" were taking upon themselves authority in the state, the Dream Team began to collapse.

The first to leave Zelensky's team was Oleksandr Danyliuk, who, since Poroshenko's presidency, had been deputy head of his administration and minister of finance. He resigned on October 27, 2019. In his post as secretary of the RNBO, he seemed like a fish out of water. Zelensky says that Danyliuk was apparently offended because he had not been made prime minister. The former secretary of the RNBO claims that the reason for his resignation was the possible reconsideration of the decision to nationalize Ihor Kolomoisky's Privatbank. He was categorically opposed to this. It seems that this position was not to the liking of the head of the Office of the President, Andriy Bohdan, who was oligarch Ihor Kolomoisky's former lawyer. Zelensky did not try to persuade Danyliuk to remain with the team.

Ruslan Ryaboshapka was the second to be "invited to leave" the Dream Team. Yes, that's right, he was invited to leave it. He had twelve years of service in the ministry of justice, headed the NABU in Mykola Azarov's government, and was a member of the newly created NAZK. On August 29, 2019, on the first working day of Ukraine's new Verkhovna Rada, he was appointed prosecutor general by a majority of the Servant of the People Party. Volodymyr Zelensky considered him "one hundred percent his man." At least that's the way Zelensky, in a conversation with Donald Trump, had described Ryaboshapka, expecting him to present first and foremost criminal cases against his opponent Petro Poroshenko. But nothing came of this. Instead, in the Verkhovna Rada a draft of a resolution of no confidence in Prosecutor General Ruslan Ryaboshapka was registered. It was signed by more than a hundred deputies from the Servant of the People Party, the Opposition Platform Za Zhyttya! (For Life!), Batkivshchyna, and the For the Future parliamentary group. The signatures demanding his resignation were collected by the people's deputy from the Servant of the People Party, Maksym Buzhansky.

The reason, as stated in the explanatory note, was the fact that "after more than six months in office, Prosecutor General Ruslan Ryaboshapka has not demonstrated any activity in investigating the illegal activities of the most highly placed government officials."

On March 4, 2020, Ryaboshapka was dismissed. Before the vote, Ryaboshapka addressed the session hall emotionally. "I did not become anyone's servant. I was and remain independent. And you cannot force an independent prosecutor to do something, you can only fire him. But I'm leaving in order to come back," Ryaboshapka summed up and demonstratively headed off toward the exit, refusing to answer questions from the people's deputies.

A few hours before the vote in the Verkhovna Rada, Zelensky called Ryaboshapka a "fine specialist" who, unfortunately, "did not produce any results." Even though he wasn't in Parliament on that particular day, but on a working trip in the Poltava region, Zelensky said: "I am sure they will say to me: ay-ay-ay, you can't touch the prosecutor general. Although, you know, he and I have been through a long haul during the election campaign. Let the deputies vote the way they want, but my personal opinion is very simple: if there are no results, he shouldn't occupy that position. And it's fair when you speak about it yourself."

Three months after his resignation, Ryaboshapka said that the way in which he was dismissed violated the "On the Prosecutor's Office" law of Ukraine: "In my personal view, the way my parting with the president happened, obviously I have certain emotions, and they are not the best. It is obvious that the way the president acted – this was probably unworthy of the rank of the president. This, perhaps, is not what would happen in civilized democracies."

Ryaboshapka would tell me later in an interview that Zelensky failed altogether to understand the role of the prosecutor general:

> He does not understand how the system of anti-corruption organs functions, to say nothing about certain specific aspects of the work of the anti-corruption infrastructure. He failed completely to understand how the criminal justice system works. When Honcharuk spoke only about the sphere of economics, that the president has fog in his head – well, in the sphere of the law the president has exactly that same kind of a fog. We tried to fight against it. We held many meetings during the election campaign, when we strove to explain how and what works, how it should

work, what the problems are today . . . But, unfortunately, for some reason it has not remained in his memory.

In this way, eleven months after Zelensky's election as president, his childhood friend Ivan Bakanov was the only one left from the Dream Team, which he widely promoted in the press.

All those who brought Zelensky to power, including those who opened the doors for him to international politics, turned out to be surplus to requirement.

Ryaboshapka states that the team that led Zelensky to victory had already become redundant after just six months. The former prosecutor general recalls:

> I don't know at what point his attitude changed or if his worldview changed. Perhaps at a time when he felt that he held power firmly enough, that there was no threat to his presidency. And he began to get rid of people who were not comfortable enough for him or not loyal enough. This happened sometime before the New Year [2020], when it became clear that his party was working; the single-party majority was voting; the law-enforcement system was in his hands; and there was no one to fear. Since that time, these changes began.

According to political strategist Serhiy Haidai, Zelensky's main problem was not just his incompetence, but also the fact that he did not recognize this. As he put it:

> Zelensky, if he was conscious of the level of his incompetence, would have created two possible scenarios. The first: in the initial months of his presidency, to gather all those who know the structure of the state apparatus of Ukraine really well and study for an hour or two every day in a special

room. He had to understand very quickly what he had taken on. And then there would have been a completely different Zelensky. I think he still doesn't understand how things work, either at the local or the central levels. He became a typical hostage of the system. It is the system that tells him how to live, that it is impossible to even move from Bankova Street, because that is not the done thing. The system told him that you can't do that without motorcades. The system told him that it was very convenient to live in a country house, although he said he would never live there. That's it. There is no more Holoborodko [from his TV series]. There is just Zelensky, to whom the system dictates what procedures there are, what rules there are, what he should do. And if he had learned at least how it all works, he would have behaved differently.

And the second Zelensky should have been like this: after studying how the system works, he should have invited specialists from outside the system, maybe even from other countries. And he should have said: "I know the architecture of power in Ukraine, but tell me, is this the right mechanism, and should it be? Because if the ruling class here was corrupt, criminal, completely immoral for twenty-nine years, could they have built a normal mechanism for the country? They have built a system that serves their criminal interests. How can it be changed?"

There is no such Zelensky.

Episode 30

Zelensky's Architect

On September 6, 2003, in the company of his friends from Kvartal 95, Oleksandr Pikalov, Serhiy Shefir, Yuriy Koryavchenkov, Olena Kravets, and his parents, Volodymyr Zelensky appeared at the Kryvyi Rih yard of Olena Kiyashko. Dressed in a light suit and tie with a bouquet in his hand, the future president was ready for the wedding ceremony.

An eight-year-long romance with his bride-to-be Olena, who studied with him in a parallel class at the Kryvyi Rih School No. 95, was coming to a resolution. Dozens of trips together to *KVK* concerts and festivals, cheerful company, and temporary times apart were behind them. Ahead of them was a life together, in which they would conquer the pinnacles of show business, and Olena would eventually become First Lady of Ukraine.

I am sure that if someone had told Olena then that her husband would become the president of Ukraine, and she would be the first lady, she would not have believed it. In 2003, at least, that looked like a utopia.

Despite attending parallel classes, Zelensky and Olena

didn't get to know each other until after graduating. He went on to study law at the Kryvyi Rih Institute of Economics, and she studied architecture at the Kryvyi Rih University. Olexandr Pikalov, an actor in Kvartal 95 and a longtime friend of Zelensky, maintains that, in order to introduce Zelensky to Olena, he asked her to lend him a video cassette to watch. And Zelensky was the one to return it. It was simply in this way that their friendship began, which later grew into an eight-year-long romance and, finally, marriage. Olena, on the other hand, remembers that everything was much easier than that: she was walking down the street with her friend, and Zelensky was walking in the opposite direction with some guys. "We lived in the same part of the city. So, bit by bit, we got to know each other, began to chat with each other, and then – started dating. At first, I wasn't ready for a relationship, but he succeeded in winning me over," she said.

Although Olena Kiyashko graduated from the university with honors, she was not destined to become an architect. Just as, in the end, Zelensky did not become a lawyer. Instead, the couple had a common interest in *KVK*, on the basis of which Kvartal 95 Studio was created. He was the artistic director, and she was one of the authors of the scripts for the *Evening Kvartal* and for the *Women's Kvartal* programs.

In 2005, Olena gave birth to a daughter, Oleksandra, and in 2013 to a son, Kyrylo. As it happens, Oleksandra was baptized by Olena Kravets's husband Serhiy, and at the same time, since Olena Zelensky was not baptized, Olena Kravets became her godmother.

The Zelensky children are enrolled at the elite Novopechersk School.

The Zelenskys' daughter has already managed to "shine" on the TV screen in the program *Make a Comedian Laugh* and star in a movie. In 2016, in her father's project, she won

50,000 hryvnias (about $1,700), which she gave to charity. His daughter's participation in the game caught Zelensky by surprise. "Before that, she and Olena had said that they wanted to try their hand at the project, but I said, 'No way!' They didn't come to the next recording of the show – that made me drop my guard, and I relaxed. And I didn't expect them to do it. Olena and one of the guys helped to prepare the jokes," he said in an interview.

Prior to the presidential election, Mrs. Zelensky was in the shadow of her husband. She avoided unnecessary publicity and was categorically opposed to her husband's participation in the election campaign. She acknowledged in an interview with Vogue.ua in November 2019:

> I am not a public person. But new realities dictate their own conditions, and I try to match expectations. I won't say that publicity or communicating with the press is stressful for me. On the other hand, I feel better backstage. My husband is always at centerstage, but I am more comfortable in the shadows. I'm not the life and soul of the party. I don't like to tell jokes. It's not my cup of tea. But I found arguments for myself in favor of the benefit of a public life. One of them is the opportunity to draw people's attention to important social issues. True, this does not apply to the public life of my children: till this day I have not posted their photos on social networks, and I will not do so now.

De jure, at the time of the election, Zelensky's wife owned 0.01 percent of Kvartal 95 Studio LLC and a quarter of Zelari Fish LLC, which processes and preserves fish, crustaceans, and mollusks as its main activity. She is also a shareholder of Aldorante Limited and a beneficiary owner of Film Heritage Inc., San Tommaso SRL. Her father, Volodymyr Kiyashko, previously managed Kryvorizhmonolitbud LLC and Technoimpulse LLC, which produce building metal structures and concrete mortars. After the victory of the Servant of the People candidates in the 2019 parliamentary elections, Kiyashko became a volunteer assistant to people's deputy Oleh Bondarenko.

Olena Zelensky apparently feared that her husband's bid for the presidency would change him, their relationship, and their lives. Better than anyone else, Olena knew her husband well, his strengths and weaknesses. That is why she hoped to the very end that he would refuse to run. "Are you crazy?" This was the first thing she asked when Zelensky began to talk about the presidency.

Olena had no idea, on December 31, 2018, that her husband was about to announce his campaign for president. She learned about it the next day from social networks. As she related to BBC Ukraine:

> We were just on a ski trip in France, calmly celebrating the New Year, drinking some champagne, and on our way to bed. In the morning I saw this flurry of activity on social networks. I was really surprised and asked him: couldn't you have warned me so I could have prepared myself mentally? And he answered, "Didn't I say anything to you? I just forgot." The fact of the matter was that they were on tour and recorded this announcement in another city after a show. We didn't see each other until the New Year, because he was on tour, and he forgot to tell me. That is why this surprise was waiting for me.

Whatever it was, it was on that New Year's Eve that Olena Zelensky's life changed. Once and for all. From the shadow of her husband, she was forced to come out onto the public stage. Her first appearance in the frame came during the nomination to the presidency of her husband by the Servant of the People Party, then she accompanied him on a trip to Paris to meet Macron, and then came a triumphant appearance on the stage of the Parkovy Conference Center on the day of Zelensky's election victory – and a thank you from her husband.

However, behind all this "gloss" was the trolling of Olena on social networks, her inclusion in the Myrotvorets[1] database the day before the election for a re-post dating back to years earlier, and Zelensky's opponents' attempts to demoralize his wife.

On April 20, 2020, the Myrotvorets site stated that Olena Zelensky was an "informant of militants of illegal armed groups" because she had posted information on her page from Russian media sources asking for information on the movements of Ukrainian troops. Olena tried to justify herself, saying that in 2014 she did not know the technical features of Facebook and that in fact she was outraged by the actions of Russian propagandists. A day later, the Myrotvorets site removed Olena Zelensky from its "blacklist."

A month later, on May 20, the day of Volodymyr Zelensky's inauguration, Olena appeared in public in a white dress designed by Artem Klimchuk. Then, as first lady, she made her debut on Instagram. Even before her husband's victory, she reiterated that she was nervous about politics and would like to remain the writer of scripts for Kvartal 95 Studio. On inauguration day, Olena's anxiety was noticeable. She sat in the guest box of the Verkhovna Rada next to four former presidents of Ukraine – Petro Poroshenko, Viktor Yushchenko, Leonid Kuchma, and Leonid Kravchuk

---

[1] Myrotvorets is a Kyiv-based Ukrainian website that publishes personal information of people who are considered to be "enemies of Ukraine," or, as the website describes itself, "Center for Research of Signs of Crimes against the National Security of Ukraine, Peace, Humanity, Security and the [sic] International Law." https://myrotvorets.center/.

– with a very serious expression on her face and she was, in all likelihood, saying farewell to her peaceful life.

Since then, Olena Zelensky's every public appearance, her clothes, her shoes, have been the subject of detailed discussion on social media. But no matter how modestly the first lady of Ukraine behaves, her husband shapes the attitude of Ukrainians toward her. From his actions, from his statements, from his successes or failures, opinions about Olena Zelensky are formed. In her new status, she strives to be a patron of culture, education, and medicine. She tries to be sincere and open. Just as her current status requires. In addition, as Volodymyr Zelensky admitted in an interview with Dmytro Gordon, when his wife is not nearby, he feels disabled. "She doesn't think she influences me much, but she does. I really trust her," he says. "I love her as much as I do myself. And when your wife gives you the gift of children, you realize that, damn, you love children even more than yourself, it's a catastrophe! I'm not ready to lose them for anything," the president confessed.

Nevertheless, Olena Zelensky weighs up her role quite modestly. She says she can quarrel with her husband and debate with him on political topics, and can support him. "He is very honest and a workaholic," is the way Olena describes him, and adds that he cannot relax. "He gives the impression that he is a jolly guy and a joker, but when we go on vacation, it is not until the third day that he cuts loose and safely looks around," she admits.

On June 12, 2020, the Office of the President of Ukraine announced that the first lady had contracted COVID-19. As was later revealed, Zelensky's 7-year-old son Kyrylo also contracted the disease.

Against this background, information began to spread in the media about the president's apparently pregnant press secretary Yuliya Mendel and their possible affair. The press cited the words of the leader of the 5.10 Party, Hennadiy Balashov, who spoke about this publicly. Mendel was forced to record a video message in which she denied all rumors about her "peculiar" condition and admitted that her mother almost had a heart attack because of these rumors. It is unknown how Olena Zelensky reacted to this. During almost the entire summer of 2020, she remained outside the public sphere. She didn't reappear with her husband until August 24, Ukrainian Independence Day.

A few days later, on August 28, Olena Zelensky posted a reminder of herself on her Instagram account. She put up a photo of an unhappy cat, which was seemingly reacting to the appearance of her fake social accounts on the Internet:

> Recently, I've come across several of "my" alleged posts or comments on social networks and Telegram channels. I understand that I have no control over this: they will appear regardless of my wishes or consent. But I really don't want any of these fakes to offend or mislead anyone.
>
> That's why – these are places on social networks you can officially find out about me.
>
> I have a page on Facebook (the post you are currently reading) and on Instagram – @olenazelenska_official. All information is "first hand" here.
>
> I don't have any other official pages on any social networks or Telegram channels, or any YouTube channel. If anything changes, I'll be sure to inform you!
>
> And thank you to all my Facebook and Instagram followers for being with me.

Undoubtedly, Olena was, and still remains, one of the architects of Zelensky's career.

Episode 31
The Magic Number 95

Volodymyr Zelensky's childhood began in Mongolia. His father, Oleksandr Semenovych, who was an engineer, was in charge of building a mining and processing plant there. The future president of Ukraine spent several years of his childhood in the small town of Erdenet. As his mother Rimma Volodymyrivna remembers – who, by the way, was also an engineer – the young Volodymyr really loved children, and they loved him. "He even used to gather children around him in kindergarten," she says.

Mongolia at that time was considered to be the sixteenth republic of the USSR. Moscow helped the People's Republic by building up a socialist economy there. The 39th Army of the Trans-Baikal Military District was based in Mongolia. The Soviet Union was preparing for a possible war with China, and the Kremlin was therefore doing everything in the Far East to create a foothold there for Soviet troops. So, besides the military, many citizens of the USSR also worked in Mongolia.

After a few years spent in Erdenet, Zelensky and his mother returned to Kryvyi Rih, while his father remained in Mongolia for a period. In Erdenet, the future president of Ukraine completed his first year at primary school. And in his second year he attended Kryvyi Rih School No. 95, which included in-depth study of English. The school later became a secondary school. By an irony of fate, the neighborhood/ block where the Zelensky family lived was also the 95th and is called the "anthill" by residents of the city. Zelensky graduated from high school in 1995. In a word, the number 95 turned out to be magical for him.

All his teachers without exception mention Zelensky as a diligent and intelligent child whose ambition was to be on stage – either as part of a choir, or as part of a dance group, or as part of a school *KVK*. Well, it would have been really strange if they had something bad to say about the sixth president of Ukraine. From his childhood, Zelensky had a bass voice (yes, that's his recognizable timbre), which prevented him from singing in the primary school choir, but it also helped him stand out from hundreds of other students.

In middle school, Zelensky had the nickname "Khammer" – at that time the singer MC Hammer was popular – and then the nickname "Zelenyi" (meaning green).

Zelensky's father wanted his son to excel in the sciences – mathematics and physics. Zelensky was drawn more to the humanities, which, of course, created conflicts with his father. As Zelensky himself recalled, his father scolded him for his poor grades in math. "A 'B' in math was a day of mourning at our house. That's not a funeral. A funeral would be a 'C'," Zelensky recalls.

The future president of Ukraine was interested in ball-room dancing, amateur performances, theater, and then *KVK*. At age 16, he received a grant to study in Israel for free, but his father was opposed to this. After graduating from high school, Zelensky did not go to the Kyiv Institute of International Relations as he had hoped. His father wanted him to have a more practical profession, such as a lawyer. Therefore, Zelensky entered the law department of the Kryvyi Rih Economic Institute at the Kyiv National Economic University, where his father taught. But, despite his father's wishes, after graduating from the university in 2000, Zelensky never worked in his field of specialization.

At Kryvyi Rih and School No. 95, Zelensky got to know Oleksandr Pikalov, Serhiy Kravets, Denys Manzhosov, and many other people who later became the main members of the Kvartal 95 Studio. Producer Oleh Chornyi and TV presenter Anatoliy Anatolych (Anatoliy Yatsechko) graduated from the same school. In short, the atmosphere in which Volodymyr Zelensky grew up was a creative one.

Zelensky used to sit at the same desk as Denys Manzhosov. In the eleventh grade (the senior year in the Ukrainian educational system), they both joined the Student Theater of Stage Miniatures "Bezpryzornyk" (Stray), whose artistic director was Oleksandr Pikalov. Childhood friends, Manzhosov and Zelensky initially followed the same life path. They studied in the same department, created a team at *KVK* Kvartal 95, and then at Kvartal 95 Studio. And it continued this way until 2013. But then the bosom buddies quarreled. Neither side will say exactly what happened to cause the quarrel. It's as if this were a purely internal matter. "I don't really feel like discussing this topic, because these kinds of moments in life are really complex and you don't very easily get through them internally. There is a lot of stress in my life, and it is difficult for me to recall what happened," Zelensky said at the time. After leaving Kvartal, Manzhosov set up his own event management agency in Kryvyi Rih, and later studied in New York for four and a half years. On April 11, 2019, he reappeared in Zelensky's life. It was on this very day that Denys Manzhosov announced a press conference called "ZadZErkallya [Behind the ZEmirror] – how and why the paths diverged of childhood best friends, Volodymyr Zelensky and Denys Manzhosov, partners in *KVK* and Kvartal 95 Studio." What this friend from his childhood and teenage years wanted to say about the future president remained a mystery, as Manzhosov did not appear before the journalists. Former friends of his, Oleksandr Pikalov and Artem Gagarin, who came to listen to him, say that money was paid to the former Kvartal participant. However, they did not specify for what exactly he was paid, or what secret Manzhosov had to reveal.

Be that as it may, it was Kryvyi Rih and School No. 95 that presented Volodymyr Zelensky not only with friends, but also with those with whom he conquered the pinnacles of show business and politics. The number 95 turned out to be magical for the sixth president of Ukraine.

Episode 32

He Who Burdened Zelensky with the Presidency

On December 15, 2015, the online newspaper *Ukrainska Pravda* published an article, "Why Zelensky Will Become the Next President." Its author was from Sumy, Viktor Bobyrenko, chief of the expert group of the Bureau of Policy Analysis, who had predicted both the appearance of the Servant of the People Party and the possibility of Zelensky's presidency four years before the triumph of the Kvartal players.

Bobyrenko was convinced it would be from the Servant of the People Party that a new twist in the spirit of paternalism in Ukraine would emerge.

However, what is striking is how, precisely five years earlier, the author had described the development of events:

Volodymyr Zelensky will end up acting in three seasons of the *Servant of the People* TV series. He will create a party. He will say that it will be like in the movies now. They will show ten or so new faces, because the old ones from [Savyk] Shuster's political talk show are already familiar. There will be a new picture.

The lines have already been memorized in the series. You don't have to come up with anything. The screenwriters of the series go into the creative department of the headquarters. Kolomoisky has the money for "our answer to Chamberlain."

And here it is also a matter of honor to get even. And we have a new president.

Who knows whether Zelensky had any thoughts about the presidency before the release of *Servant of the People* on the screen. But we should not exclude the idea that such thoughts may have surfaced after the text written by Viktor Bobyrenko, which was commented on by everyone after the presidential election and the stunning victory of the artistic director of Kvartal 95 Studio.

Although, as political strategist Serhiy Haidai said to me, after the astounding success of the *Servant of the People* series, lawyers who worked with Volodymyr Zelensky asked him for advice about the creation of a new political project. Haidai told me:

I have long been friends with Mykola Katerynchuk. His law firm for a long time has provided legal services to Kvartal 95 Studio. At that time, Mykola was friends with Zelensky and invited me to meet him. It was possible that Kvartal could take part in some kind of election campaigns – given that they mimicked and parodied politicians. At that time the meeting did not take place. Later, several lawyers left Katerynchuk and set up their own company, which began working with Kvartal. And one day they came to me and said: "We have a client. He wants to go into politics, but he's really distant from it. And he doesn't want everyone to know about it. Would you like to advise him?" I tried to find out who it was. They wouldn't tell me. We called it a day. Then I noticed these lawyers among Zelensky's associates – Vadym Halaichuk, who represented Volodymyr's interests in the CEC and later became a people's deputy of Ukraine, and Serhiy Nyzhniy, managing partner of Hillmont Partners.

It seems that among those who then approached the founder of GAIDAYCOM (Haidai) was another lawyer, Ivan Bakanov, who, after Zelensky's victory in the presidential election, would be in charge of the SBU. Ivan described in an interview with BBC Ukraine in spring 2019 how they turned to Haidai at a stage when the Servant of the People Party was of no interest to anyone.

In short, since 2015, Zelensky's team had been trying hard to decide whether to enter into politics. Although, as the aforementioned Viktor Bobyrenko said, Kvartal has always been an instrument for destroying Ihor Kolomoisky's opponents:

> When I watched two seasons of *Servant of the People* and heard from an acquaintance: "If only we had such a president!" I realized that this Kvartal has become an instrument for taking power. I am a specialist in the study of the mind. I also wrote a candidate's degree dissertation [PhD] on this topic – "The Dynamic State of Contemporary Ethnic Groups." I made a bold prognosis, and, unfortunately for me, it came true. Someone tells me that it was I who provoked them into taking this step – entering into politics. I don't think so. Because when they saw the overwhelming success of the series, they realized that Vova [Zelensky] can be used for more than just "a rubout."

Victor is convinced that interest in a decent politician in Ukraine has been and remains sufficiently high, something of which, in fact, Volodymyr Zelensky, playing the role of Vasyl Holoborodko (in his TV series), took advantage. Bobyrenko told me:

> This seemingly simple technology worked. And this happened because no one, including Petro Poroshenko, saw Zelensky as a competitor. You remember how at that time he "crushed" Andriy Sadovy with Lviv garbage, then fought with Yuliya Tymoshenko? Until the New Year of 2019, he was set to do battle with the leader of the Batkivshchyna Party. But since Ihor Kolomoisky was playing with chutzpah, Zelensky also began to play boldly during the presidential campaign. Remember how, during the debate at the stadium, he slapped Poroshenko on the back and pressed him with words like "thiiink!" However, this style in time played a wicked joke on Zelensky. Because it didn't take long before he was publicly being called "Bubochka," "Vovochka," and "Zelya."

This wasn't the first time the citizen from Sumy saw into the future regarding Zelensky – and it wasn't the last. In 2011, he predicted the next Maidan, and in 2008, when Putin was a popular politician in Ukraine, Bobyrenko predicted that he would lose the Ukrainian state.

Well, the next president of Ukraine, according to Bobyrenko, will be . . . Vitaliy Klitschko. Yes, the former world boxing champion. And he explains why:

> In order for someone to be president, a consensus among the oligarchs is needed. And, unfortunately for Ukraine, Vitaliy Klitschko is not as aggressive in politics as he was as a boxer. He knows how to bargain. But if Akhmetov, Pinchuk, Firtash from Vienna, and Avakov agree, they will bet on Klitschko. However, the mayor of Dnipro, Borys Filatov, shouldn't be excluded. Because you need not only

to have a consensus among the oligarchs. You also need to knock off Zelensky. Filatov is able to do this beautifully and more harmoniously. I'd like to see Poroshenko's political reincarnation. But this is unlikely to happen.

Whether or not Viktor Bobyrenko's prediction about Klitschko comes true will become apparent in just a few years. In two years, anything can happen in Ukraine, in spite of Zelensky's substantial popular support during the Russo-Ukrainian war. As it happens, the mayor of the capital, along with his brother Volodymyr, has also proved to be a fighter during the Russian aggression. He defended Kyiv from the aggressors. However, whatever happens in the 2024 elections, political strategist Viktor Bobyrenko will forever remain in our memory as the man who, way back in 2015, predicted the presidency for Zelensky and the triumph of the Servant of the People Party. And he is one of the few who can say to all of us: "I told you so!"

Episode 33

A Gagarin for Zelensky

On October 25, 2020, the first local elections for the presidential party Servant of the People took place in Ukraine. De facto, this completed the process of decentralization in the country. Following the introduction of administrative reform and the consolidation of districts, the number of local deputies in Ukraine decreased by 30 percent, and organs of self-government were reconstituted into full-fledged proprietors and managers of local budgets.

After two spectacular election campaigns in 2019, the Servant of the People Party hoped for victory in local elections as well. However, against all expectations, the presidential team lost the mayoral elections in the largest cities of Ukraine – in Kyiv, Dnipro, Odesa, Kharkiv, and Lviv. Yes, the "servants" received representation in the regions, but results there fell far short of the 73 percent of votes won in the presidential election and the 43 percent in the parliamentary election.

Zelensky's allies understood that they would have to share power in the country with other political forces and regional leaders. The period of single-party power was over.

Two weeks before the local elections, on October 25, Zelensky – to everyone's surprise – initiated a so-called nationwide survey.

Presenting five questions for discussion to Ukrainians, the president wanted to convince voters that their opinion was very important to him, above all else. However, he did it very unconvincingly. The questions concerned the introduction of life imprisonment for large-scale corruption, the creation of a free economic zone in the Donbas, a reduction in the number of deputies in the Verkhovna Rada to 300, the legalization of medical cannabis, and taking the discussion of security guarantees set out in the Budapest Memorandum to an international level.

As a result, Zelensky's opponents accused him of attempting to campaign illegally for the Servant of the People Party on election day, which, in fact, took on the financing of this rather strange survey. And Artem Gagarin, the showman and music producer of Kvartal 95, took care of it. Yes, Gagarin. Putin had Tereshkova, and Zelensky had Gagarin.

It is difficult to say what Zelensky really wanted – to bolster the rating of his party or, for example, to enlist the support of Ukrainians for the creation of a free economic zone in the Donbas. But we have to admit that the survey failed. This is evidenced by the extremely poor organization of the process, the sharp criticism of the poll by opponents, and the doubtful numbers of those who agreed to complete the survey, which the presidential team would eventually receive. Exit polls indicated a low level of voter interest. A third of those who took part just ignored the pollsters. And in light of the relatively low voter turnout (only about 37 percent of eligible participants), it was immediately clear that the results would be meaningless.

Zelensky promised Ukrainians that the results of the survey would allow the authorities to prepare the necessary legislation for consideration in the Verkhovna Rada. But Artem Gagarin and the action conducted by him on the day of the local elections completely discredited the idea of rule by the people in this format, and therefore, naturally questions were asked. For example, who was responsible for conducting a survey not provided for by current Ukrainian legislation? How and by whom would the results of the pseudo-referendum be used? What will Zelensky do if other political parties conduct similar fake polls? There are still no answers to these questions. It is doubtful that anyone will mention this survey again after the war.

But it is quite obvious that, after Ukraine's victory in the war with Russia, we will see a completely different Zelensky, "servants of the people," and the ways in which they operate with Ukrainians.

Zelensky needs a new Gagarin. But, perhaps, he will become this Gagarin himself.

Episode 34

A Black Mirror for a Hero

The morning of July 21, 2020 turned out to be sunny and warm in Kyiv.

There was no sense of foreboding.

The capital was going through another summer day of quarantine. The center of the city suffered from traffic jams. Children and their mothers were playing in the parks of Kyiv. And Zelensky was preparing for a meeting with the president of the Swiss Confederation Simonetta Sommaruga. The state flags of both countries were flapping in the courtyard of the Mariinsky Palace, a guard of honor was lined up there, and artillerymen were preparing to fire a twenty-one-gun salute in honor of the guests.

At the same time, four hundred kilometers from the capital, in Lutsk, a drama was unfolding.

An armed man had seized a passenger bus and declared the day Antisystem Day. He handcuffed the hostages to their seats and threatened to blow up the bus containing thirteen passengers. Twice-convicted Maksym Kryvosh (known online as Maksym Plokhoy [Maksym the Bad]) presented an ultimatum to the president and top Ukrainian politicians.

The former was to record a video and recommend that Ukrainians watch Shaun Monson's film *Earthlings* (2005) about the suffering of animals at the hands of humans. The politicians were to publish on their social media pages confessions that they were "terrorists according to the law." Well then, why not tell the story of one of the episodes of the *Black Mirror* TV series, when an unknown assailant kidnaps British Princess Susannah and forces the prime minister to make love to a pig on live TV?

Apparently, realizing the absurdity of Kryvosh's demands, Zelensky was visibly nervous during his meeting with the Swiss president, commenting on the events in Lutsk. There were several breaks during the negotiations.

Interior minister Arsen Avakov, deputy head of the Office of the President Kyrylo Tymoshenko, and heads of law-enforcement agencies had already flown there to negotiate with the terrorist. The criminal's demands appeared insane. This is why rumors started to circulate about his treatment in a mental hospital. Truth be told, this was not confirmed later. But it became known that he is the author of the book *Philosophy of a Criminal*, which contains the following lines: "They have been trying to fix me for 15 years, but I haven't been fixed, but just the opposite. I have become even more of who I am. Why? Because I'm managing myself and that's why I won't be managed by others . . . There is only one thing I can't do – not be a criminal. I can, because I decide everything myself and live in my own way."

Almost all day, the police tried to persuade Kryvosh to release the hostages. He was relentless, insisting on his demands being met.

At 9 p.m., Zelensky posted a video on his Facebook page with a very brief summary: "The 2005 film *Earthlings*. A must-see!" Prior to that, it turned out that the president had spoken to Kryvosh for seven minutes and persuaded him to release at least three of the hostages – a pregnant woman, a child, and a wounded man (who, as it turned out, was not on the bus).

After half an hour, Kryvosh turned himself in to the police. Quietly, peacefully, and without any resistance. The president deleted his video from Facebook. The twelve-hour hostage epic ended successfully: the hostages were released; Kryvosh was put in jail, and the leadership of the country, headed by Volodymyr Zelensky, had complied with the demands of the terrorist.

However, the course of events, and, most importantly, their outcome, left many questions – both for the special services and for the president in control of them. Because Ukrainian special services ended up among the victims. First, they were not able to prevent the taking of hostages, and then they failed to conduct an operation to release them.

The attempted terrorist attack in Lutsk was the third in President Zelensky's term. Prior to that, twice, on September 18, 2019 and June 1, 2020, there were threats to blow up the Metro Bridge in Kyiv, which would have paralyzed the capital.

Each "mine-layer" had his own motive. But they all had one thing in common – the situation was invariably settled by interior minister Arsen Avakov and his subordinates. It happened that way in Kyiv. It happened that way in Lutsk. This, in fact, allowed some Ukrainians to say that these terrorist attacks were nothing more than a show. They say that, in this way, Avakov was flexing his "muscles" and behaving like, if not the first, then at least the second in charge in Ukraine.

After the incident in Lutsk, Zelensky himself stated that, despite his high rank, he was and remains a human being. "I live with these principles, I have lived with them, I will live with them – to become president and remain a human being. We have a positive result – everyone is alive. We are not fighting for ratings – we are fighting for lives. And for me, this is the most important principle."

Zelensky, despite being ridiculed by his opponents, did everything in his power to save people. And, probably, this is how the story of the Lutsk terrorist will be remembered.

Episode 35

Zvirobiy, Fedyna, and a Victim

At the end of October 2019, President Zelensky was preparing the Ukrainian army for a retreat of forces from Zolote and Petrivske in the Donbas. This was one of the preconditions Vladimir Putin laid down for him to agree to attend the Normandy Four summit in Paris, which the Ukrainian head of state very much wanted to happen.

On October 26, Zelensky traveled to Zolote. There, in the style of Vasyl Holoborodko (his TV presidential character), he spoke to the peaceful inhabitants and strove to gain their support. The conversation followed the approach taken by Mikhail Gorbachev (former Soviet leader), who loved to hear what the people had to say just before the plenums and congresses of the Central Committee of the CPSU. "We will act from above, and you give pressure from below," the first and last president of the USSR loved to repeat. And what did Zelensky want to hear from the inhabitants of Zolote, some of whom had not always been opposed to the idea of a so-called "New Russia" – except for the fact that the Donbas was in need of peace?

However, in contrast to Gorbachev, an unpleasant meeting with Donbas war veterans, who had organized a "No to Capitulation" demonstration, awaited Zelensky. They were sure that another deployment of armed forces along the line of confrontation would lead to an exacerbation of the conflict at the front.

Zelensky's conversation with the veterans was prickly. One of the guys, named Denys, asked the president if he was planning to talk to the veterans and explain his position regarding the towns of Zolote and Petrovske. Zelensky replied with irritation: "Listen, I'm the president of this country. I'm going to be 42 years old. I'm not some kind of total douche. I came to you and told you to put away your weapons. Stop pulling the wool over my eyes. I wanted to see understanding in your eyes. But instead I saw a guy who decided that a schmoe was standing in front of him and who was pulling the wool over my eyes."

It is understood that Zelensky wanted to show exactly who was in charge in the Donbas. But the conduct, style, and manner of communication of the commander-in-chief were strange. And this can only be explained by the insecurity he felt in his actions.

Everyone has probably already forgotten this conversation, so the story goes no further.

The Ukrainian volunteer and enlisted soldier Marusya Zvirobiy (Olena Bilenka), along with the people's deputy from the European Solidarity Party Sofia Fedyna, came out live on Facebook and, rather coarsely, using selective obscenities, commented on Zelensky's behavior. They warned him that one cannot talk to veterans like that, because anything could happen to the president in the Donbas – a nearby grenade explosion, a chance bombardment, etc. In other words, the president should not think that he's immortal.

"They'll blow you up. I promise you. You keep traveling over there more often. But the dudes weren't morally ready for you today. They even addressed you with the respectful 'Vy' [you, second person plural] form. You need, dog, to get soaked in the latrine. That's what Putin said about people like you," wrote Zvirobiy.

The HPU and the DBR, based on threats against the president, demanded the removal of Fedyna's parliamentary immunity, and instituted criminal proceedings against her under three articles: actions regarding the forcible change or overthrow of the constitutional order or seizure of state power (Article 109, part 3), an attempt on the life of a governmental or public figure (Article 112), and the threat or violence against a governmental or public figure (Article 346).

And then, Marusya Zvirobiy's home was searched, as a result of which three cellphones and two hunting rifles were found. Both women were summoned to the DBR. Because of Fedyna's and Zvirobiy's threats, Zelensky complained to the DBR, calling himself a victim.

It must be said that the case of Fedyna and Zvirobiy is not unique to Ukrainian politics. Under Zelensky's three predecessors, law-enforcement organs also endeavored to find those who apparently wanted to assassinate those particular presidents. In 2004, they searched for the person who poisoned Viktor Yushchenko, but he was never found. In 2013, activists from Sumy were convicted of drawing images of President Yanukovych with a bullet through his head. And in 2016, the activist Yuriy Pavlenko, nicknamed "Khort" (wolfhound), was sentenced to four and a half years in prison (although he was later released) for publicly tearing up a portrait of President Poroshenko during a protest.

Under the Poroshenko regime, the Office of the Prosecutor General reported on the discovery of the activities of two groups that were apparently preparing a coup d'état in Ukraine. Former Georgian President Mikheil Saakashvili led one, according to the HPU. Former Ukrainian army pilot, POW, people's deputy, and hero of Ukraine Nadiya Savchenko led the second. Admittedly, the guilt of neither Saakashvili nor Savchenko has ever been confirmed in a Ukrainian court.

On February 10, 2020, the Pechersk District Court of Kyiv chose a precautionary measure for Marusya Zvirobiy – on her own recognizance she was not permitted to leave Kyiv and the Kyiv region for two months and had to wear an electronic ankle bracelet. After three months, the court did not extend the precautionary measure, although the investigation into Zvirobiy and Fedyna continued for two more months.

This is how this entire story, which had long drawn the attention of Zelensky's opponents, ended.

Episode 36

Wagnergate: A Story with Many Unknowns

Since mid-2020, Zelensky's Achilles heel has been Wagnergate. This entire time, the leadership of the Ukrainian state has told the public various stories about a special operation employed to detain members of the Wagner PVK (Private Military Company). At first, they tried to prove that this special operation was pure fiction. Then, that it was the work of Moscow. And later, that the plan to capture the cutthroats who fought in the Donbas threatened the safety of other people. In short, it went from complete denial through indignation to the acknowledgment that such a special operation really took place.

Everything began on July 29, 2020. Belarusian special services, fearful of being provoked by Russian special services on the eve of the Belarusian presidential election, detained thirty-three members of the Wagner PVK in a hotel near Minsk. The fighters, who had fought in various parts of the world, including the Donbas, were preparing to depart for Istanbul, and then – to Venezuela. There, according to the official version, they were intending to work as security guards on oil company rigs. Later, however, it turned out that all this – both the recruiting and the attempt to lure the "Wagnerites" from Russia – was part of a larger game of the Ukrainian special services. Postponement of this special operation for several days (according to one version, the leadership of the Ukrainian state did not want to squabble with the Russians on the eve of a publicized truce in the Donbas) led to a sad finale.

For several years, officers of the SBU and the HUR MO (Chief Office of Intelligence of the Ministry of Defense) had been collecting documents and proof of the participation of Wagner PVK members in the war in the Donbas. Of the thirty-three Wagnerites detained in Belarus, thirteen were involved in Russian crimes in eastern Ukraine in 2014–15. This included fighting in the battalion of the Russian writer Zakhar Prilepin, who has himself publicly confirmed this.

The SBU confirms that those arrested in Minsk had been involved in the downing of a Ukrainian IL-76 military transport plane, shot down at Luhansk Airport in 2014, and were also involved in attacking the airport and in battles for the eastern Ukrainian town of Debaltseve. The plan to detain the Wagnerites on Ukrainian territory (as a result of a forced emergency landing of the plane on its way from Minsk to Istanbul) was supposed to become the final chapter in this story. However, this special operation under the code name Avenue to have Belarus detain important participants in Russia's bloody war was foiled.

Immediately after the detention of the Wagnerites, Zelensky publicly requested that Belarusian President Lukashenko turn over those arrested to Ukraine. In an interview with the journalist Dmytro Gordon, he promised to do this. However, he failed to keep his word. The Wagnerites went back to Russia, and Ukraine ended up with Wagnergate. After the failure of the special operation, the head of the ministry of defense, Vasyl Burba, was dismissed.

He did not hide his outrage, and the officers who prepared the special operation were fired from their jobs.

When the details of Operation Avenue appeared in the press, the Office of the President for a long time denied the fact that any such exercise had been conducted. This prompted the opposition to accuse Zelensky and his team of leaking information to the Belarusians and Russians. According to them, Zelensky and his circle consciously wrecked Operation Avenue, making them accomplices of the Kremlin.

At the end of 2020, Bellingcat investigators began to ask questions. Hristo Grozev's team collected information about this special operation over the course of a year. In summer 2021, Zelensky spoke in one of his interviews about the details of Operation Avenue. And a special commission of the Verkhovna Rada, headed by a representative of the Servant of the People Party Maryana Bezuhla, came to the conclusion that neither Yermak nor Zelensky was implicated in the breakdown of the special operation.

A year later, on November 17, 2021, Bellingcat published the results of its investigation. They did not directly point to treason – the transfer of information about Operation Avenue to the Russian side. Journalists described in detail the chronology of the preparation and the failure of the operation. At the same time, the former head of the HUR MO, Vasyl Burba, together with the officers who took part in working out the plan of the special operation, publicly announced the existence of a Russian mole in President Zelensky's office. And the previously mentioned journalist Yuriy Butusov accused the head of the Committee on Questions of Intelligence, Ruslan Demchenko, of working for Russia. According to him, the responsibility for this lies at the feet of Volodymyr Zelensky and his chief of staff Andriy Yermak.

The president of Ukraine says that everything concerning the special operation was Burba's personal mission. They say the latter was a protégé of Petro Poroshenko, and that is why the entire plan was an attempt by the former head of the HUR MO to get Zelensky to clash with the global community, especially Turkey, where the Wagnerites were traveling.

It is significant that, with the beginning of the Russian invasion of Ukraine, Wagnergate came to nothing. Those in the Ukrainian government who were suspected of being agents of the Kremlin squared up to Putin's challenge (i.e., the invasion) and have defended the Ukrainian state. Moreover, they are leading the resistance of the Ukrainian people. And this surely is the unexpected finale of Wagnergate. A finale that must be taken into consideration after the victory of Ukraine over Russia.

Episode 37

How the Oligarch Akhmetov Prepared a Coup for Zelensky

O n September 23, 2021, the Verkhovna Rada passed a law on the status of oligarchs. With this, Zelensky asserted, the priorities in the complex relation-ship between the state and those who are called oligarchs in Ukraine would be set once and for all. Or, to put this more accurately, Zelensky's own relationship with them. Beginning in May 2022, a corresponding register would begin to operate in the state. It would contain information about where the big money is, indicate whose business was cornering the markets, and show how their influence extends to Ukrainian politics and the media.

Zelensky's initiative triggered expected opposition from the oligarchs. Zelensky did not take into account one thing when he deployed his anti-oligarchic campaign: Ihor Kolomoisky, Rinat Akhmetov, Viktor Pinchuk, and others had endured the "bad 1990s" and five presidents of Ukraine. And they were not just planning to give up. They would sell and buy their property, including the media, several times through others or third parties offshore – and by May 2022 they would sadly declare their bankruptcy. One should not expect people who have invested hundreds of millions of dollars in the media to simply surrender to Zelensky.

It is noteworthy that a few months after the law was passed, President Zelensky announced that on December 1–2 a coup d'état was being prepared in Ukraine with the involvement of the oligarch Rinat Akhmetov and Russia. In his words, intelligence and "audio information" existed about attempts to draw the oligarch into the process of overthrowing the Ukrainian government. After Zelensky's words, the DTEK Energo company's value of eurosecurities that belonged to Akhmetov fell by 11.6 percent.

Just before this, representatives of the Servant of the People Party refused to take part in broadcasts on the Ukraine and Ukraine 24 channels, which were owned by Akhmetov. Hardly anyone guessed that Zelensky would publicly accuse Akhmetov of plotting a coup. I am certain that the oligarch himself, who started his business in the turbulent 1990s in the Donbas, did not expect it. It's worth noting that for the last thirty years he had always been on common ground with all the Ukrainian presidents. Zelensky turned out to be the exception.

Only Akhmetov and Zelensky themselves know exactly what happened between them. Unfortunately, Zelensky did not specify why Akhmetov, whose companies had, until recently, been leaders in paying their taxes in the country, turned out to be an enemy of the Ukrainian state. He failed to provide any strong evidence of the oligarch's involvement in the alleged coup.

Literally a day before Russia's massive assault against Ukraine, Zelensky gathered together fifty of the most influential businessmen, especially those considered oligarchs. The president requested that they help financially in the stand against Russia. The business holding company of Akhmetov publicly announced that it would be willing to pay one billion hryvnias (about $34 million) into the state budget in advance.

The war with Russia pushed both the de-oligarchization movement and the misunderstanding between Zelensky and Akhmetov into the background. Because everyone in Ukraine today, without exception, has just one enemy, the victory over which the existence of the Ukrainian state depends.

Episode 38

The Bucha Massacre

On May 20, 2019, on Zelensky's inauguration day, he promised the Ukrainian people that he would become Ukraine's best president. "Over the course of my life," he said, "I have tried to do everything possible to make Ukrainians smile. That was my mission. Now I will do everything possible so that Ukrainians at least do not cry." Obviously, at that time Zelensky had no way of knowing how many tears would be shed in Ukraine in 2022. Or the fact that, dressed in olive green, he would be the leader of a great nation that would take on the battle against the Russians.

On February 24, 2022, the boots of Russian soldiers brought death, torture, rape, looting, and devastation into Ukrainian homes. On that day, the lives of Ukrainians, including Zelensky's, changed. Once and for all.

Even before the start of the war with Russia, opponents of Ukraine's sixth president questioned his courage and capability of standing up to Putin and his army. They were mistaken and underestimated Zelensky. He turned out to be a "tough cookie." Few if any believed in the fighting abilities of the president, who had been a show business star three years earlier and didn't have a clue what the Ukrainian army was or how the president should conduct himself. It's said that in the first days of the war, when Western leaders suggested he should evacuate Kyiv, Zelensky answered: "I need ammunition, not a ride." At this time we don't know for certain if that really happened.

However, we have become witnesses to the way in which, since the beginning of the war, Zelensky's rhetoric has changed in the international arena. He stopped being a diplomat. He began to tell the world the truth about Russia's war against Ukraine. The president of Ukraine blamed Europe and, in particular, Germany for purchasing Russian gas from Putin and he invited Western leaders to see for themselves the consequences of the Russian occupation of the outskirts of Irpin.

Zelensky is no longer playing the role of president. He is the leader of a nation that, with weapons in its hands, is defending its freedom and independence. A leader who knows the value of every human life. A leader who has gained extensive experience in governing his country under wartime conditions. Not a single European leader has had that experience. And in a world of presidents who stand against aggression – there are only a few. Obviously, this is what allows Zelensky to speak harshly, strictly, and emotionally on the international stage, and, in return, Ukraine receives military and humanitarian aid from abroad.

Zelensky's speeches before the UN and the parliaments of different countries will most likely be studied later in history departments at institutes of higher education around the world. And his addresses to the public, which he began to videotape in Kyiv from the very first day of the war, will be an example for politicians of how to talk to the people.

"Great nation!," "Unbreakable people of the most coura-
geous country!," "Eternal glory to all who defend the state!,"
"We will remember for eternity every man and woman who
has died for Ukraine!," "Thank you to all our male defenders!
Thank you to all our women defenders!" These words of
Zelensky reverberate daily in his addresses to the nation,
uniting Ukrainians and giving everyone a sense of being part
of a single Ukrainian family.

From the first moment of the full-scale invasion, the
Russians began to kill with cruise missiles fired from the
Black Sea. They struck Kyiv, Odesa, Lviv, Lutsk, Poltava,
and Sumy. Russian fighter jets bombed residential areas in
Mariupol, Chernihiv, Kharkiv, Okhtyrka, Bucha, Irpin, and
hundreds of other small towns and villages, reducing them
to ashes. Ukraine has not suffered such devastating ruin
since World War II.

On March 31, the crimes and extraordinary brutality of
Russian soldiers in two towns near Kyiv – Bucha and Irpin
– came to light. On that day, Putin's army was driven from
the outskirts of Irpin, an area located twenty kilometers
from Kyiv. At the same time, the shooting of civilian cars
by Russian tanks, the mass murder of handcuffed adults
and children who were shot in the back of the head came
to light. In the small town of Bucha alone, the bodies of
more than three hundred people are buried in mass graves.
The invaders ran over with tanks the women they had
raped, and raped young children right in front of their
parents.

The tragedy in Bucha, which was exposed to the entire
world, is astonishing for its brutality, which cannot lend
itself to any explanation or justification. Except for just
one thing – Moscow is deliberately destroying Ukrainians.
As has occurred many times in history, when Russia
starved Ukraine, executed the Ukrainian intelligentsia,

and imprisoned Ukrainians for what the Soviets called the "bourgeois nationalism" of those who dreamt of an independent state.[1]

Volodymyr Zelensky publicly accused Russia of genocide of the Ukrainian people. Instead, Moscow continues to call Ukraine's sixth president, who was born to a Jewish family, a Nazi. This gives serious grounds for doubting the mental stability of the master of the Kremlin and his team. They, by the way, subjected Babyn Yar in Kyiv to rocket attacks, the site where Nazis executed Jews during World War II.

On April 5, after the publication of information regarding the Bucha massacre (the world's leading media outlets called it this), Zelensky delivered one of his strongest speeches before the UN Security Council. In an online delivery, he spoke emotionally about the crimes of the Russian occupiers:

> They shot women standing behind the doors of houses when they approached and simply called to see if someone was still alive. They killed entire families – both the adults and children. And they tried to burn their bodies. They killed people with a shot in the back of the head or in the eye after they had tortured them. They just shot people at random on the streets. They were tossed into wells for them to die

---

[1] This refers to the Holodomor famine, when some 5 million Ukrainians were intentionally starved to death on Stalin's orders in 1932–3. For detailed information on this, see Robert Conquest's book *Harvest of Sorrow*, or Anne Appelbaum's *Red Famine*, or the documentary film *Harvest of Despair*, the latter of which is available on YouTube. Stalin directed vicious assaults on the Ukrainian intelligentsia mostly in the 1920s and 1930s. Ukrainian cultural historians call this the Executed Renaissance, when approximately 750 Ukrainian cultural and political figures were killed, imprisoned, or committed suicide because of impending arrest. During and following the 1960s, proponents of Ukrainian culture in the USSR were subject to secret or show trials and summarily sent to the Gulag on a typically trumped-up charge of bourgeois nationalism.

suffering. They killed people in apartments, in houses, blowing them up with grenades. They crushed civilian cars with their tanks in the middle of the road. For fun. They cut off limbs, cut throats. They raped and killed people in front of their families.

This truth shocked not only the UN Security Council, but the entire world, which, until then, had watched the war in Ukraine like a Netflix series. Zelensky's testimony sobered many people. He proposed to the Security Council that it deprive Russia of its veto, or else it should disband. Lamenting the helplessness and outmoded nature of the UN, Zelensky said what everyone in the world had known for a long time but was afraid to say. However, Zelensky's stories from the high podium did not stop Putin. On April 8, the Russians launched a Tochka Y rocket attack on the Kramatorsk Railway Station, where many people had gathered, fleeing the war. More than fifty people were killed and more than a hundred injured.

Mariupol was a beautiful and thriving city on the shores of the Sea of Azov. Before the war, half a million people lived there. By day forty-five of the war, Putin had turned the city into Stalingrad. In 2014, Mariupol had been recaptured by the Ukrainian army. At that time, the inhabitants said "no" to the "Russian Spring." For this, the Russians are taking revenge on the unconquered people, destroying buildings, maternity hospitals, shopping centers, daycare centers, and schools in Mariupol. With rockets, enemy aircraft bombed the drama theater, in the basement of which people were hiding. Since then, more than three hundred people have been found dead under the rubble. Not even the inscription "ДЕТИ" (CHILDREN), written in large letters in Russian at the front and back of the theater, stopped the pilots from bombing it. Another 100,000 Mariupol residents were totally blockaded. They were without water, without electricity, without food. People buried their relatives and neighbors in the ground next to their homes and in children's playgrounds. Mobile Russian crematoria burned the dead in order to cover up their war crimes. Against this backdrop, soldiers of the Azov Regiment and Marines heroically held off the advance of 10,000 Russian troops, who were besieging Mariupol.

With the beginning of the war, Zelensky became an active player in world politics, whose words now influence both the future of the UN and the actions of leaders of various states. During the first fifty-three days of the war, Zelensky addressed most European parliaments, including the US Congress, the Knesset of Israel, and the Parliament and government of Canada. Dressed not in a suit and tie, but in a khaki green T-shirt, he was greeted and accompanied by applause and standing ovations – a sign of respect for him and the Ukrainian people. Zelensky also delivered a video address at the 64th Grammy Awards ceremony, and called for musicians to support Ukraine in the battle against Russia.

In Kyiv on April 9, Zelensky received the UK prime minister Boris Johnson, who publicly called the Ukrainian president his friend. After their discussions, they walked together through the center of the Ukrainian capital. They were accompanied, of course, by security guards. Against the backdrop of Putin hiding somewhere in the Urals in a bunker, this military promenade represented a demonstration of strength of spirit and a public slap in the face to the master of the Kremlin.

An extraordinarily difficult responsibility had been heaped on Zelensky: to lead the Ukrainian people through a war. With tears of despair, rage, and hatred for the occupiers. With faith in victory and grieving for the dead. Yes, this is

not what he dreamt about when he received the ceremonial
presidential mace (the symbol of his power and authority).
But these tribulations showed us the real Zelensky. Without
any greasepaint.

Epilogue
The President of War

Since 2019, Volodymyr Zelensky has sought to become the president of peace. He promised to end the war in the Donbas and to put an end to the thorny relations with the Russian Federation. For this, as he said, he is ready even to negotiate with the devil. However, the devil in the Kremlin was prepared to negotiate with Zelensky on just one thing – the capitulation of Ukraine to Russia. That is something to which Zelensky could not agree.

Thus, Putin left Zelensky no choice. He was forced to become the president of war rather than the president of peace. He had a complicated mission – to lead his country into battle against the Russian occupiers. This is a difficult ordeal for someone who has never served in the army and who had no experience in politics until 2019.

Prior to the war, almost every one of Zelensky's public addresses was reminiscent of his acting past. Pauses, facial expressions, tone of voice, and gestures. There was too much theatricality and artificiality in all this. It included professional video shoots of the president, with the presentation and delivery of news carried out according to show business rules. It all looked unnatural and insincere. Beginning on February 24, 2022, the first day of Russia's war against Ukraine, all this would disappear from Zelensky's arsenal. We would see a completely different person. With a weary and unshaven face. In khaki green clothing, without a tie, no makeup, or TV spotlights. A president who speaks painfully about Ukrainians in all walks of life who had fallen into the vortex of the Russo-Ukrainian war. A person with real emotions. A leader of the Ukrainian nation who will call out to the world about the war in his land.

Today, standing behind Zelensky, there is a united, strong, and invincible Ukrainian society. No one in Ukraine has ever seen such unity of the people as during this blood-shedding war with Russia. Hundreds of thousands of Ukrainians have taken up arms. Millions of people have set out to help those who stand at the front and those who have lost their homes. The war with Russia has transformed into a real people's war.

In the Ukrainian state, people have traditionally always been divided between those who have defended its independence and those who have worshiped Moscow. Between those who attended the Orthodox Church of Ukraine and those who attended branches of the Russian Orthodox Church. Between those who spoke Ukrainian and those who believed they were persecuted as a Russian-speaker. Volodymyr Zelensky's predecessors searched for a formula that would unite the entire country. But neither Leonid Kravchuk, nor Leonid Kuchma, nor Viktor Yushchenko, nor Viktor Yanukovych, nor Petro Poroshenko succeeded in doing this. This was done for them by Vladimir Putin, who started his war against Ukraine. Hatred of the Russians and their leader felt by Ukrainians today is turning the people into an invincible army. The Kremlin was certain that it would take them three or four days to conquer Ukraine. It was wrong.

No one knows exactly how and when this war will end. Just as no one knows what Ukraine will be like after the war. But, without a doubt, Ukrainians will play a significant role both in Europe and in the world.

Unfortunately, we have suffered heavy losses. Many people have died. Our cities and infrastructure have been destroyed. But the spirit of Ukrainians who are demonstrating their desire to be free and independent and who believe that Russia, just like its flagship missile cruiser *Moskva*, will follow the path directed by the Ukrainian military, remains unbreakable. Because it was from this ship that, in the first days of this war, came the demand that the border guards from Snake Island surrender. In response to that demand, they heard: "Russian ship, go screw yourself!"

The sixth president of Ukraine has come a long way – from an actor to the leader of the Ukrainian nation. From a man who was met with interest and irony by leaders of the world's nations, to a politician who is now met with applause in the West, and by world leaders who consider it an honor to call him their friend.

April 17, 2022
Kyiv–Lviv

Chronology

January 25, 1978: Volodymyr Zelensky was born in Kryvyi Rih.

1985: The USSR, under President Mikhail Gorbachev, introduced "perestroika" (restructuring, reconstruction), the purpose of which was to implement political and economic reforms. This led to an exacerbation of tensions in all spheres of life in the country, to the liquidation of the authority of the CPSU and, in **1991**, to the collapse of the Soviet Union.

August 24, 1991: The Verkhovna Rada of the Ukrainian Soviet Socialist Republic adopted the Act on the Proclamation of Independence of Ukraine.

December 1, 1991: Following the restoration of independence, Leonid Kravchuk was elected Ukraine's first president.

July 10, 1994: Leonid Kuchma was elected president of

Ukraine; he was re-elected for a second presidential term in 1999.

December 5, 1994: Ukraine signed the Budapest Memorandum. Ukraine received security guarantees from Russia, the United Kingdom, and the United States in exchange for non-nuclear status.

1995: Zelensky graduated from high school in Kryvyi Rih. Afterward, he studied in the law department at the Kyiv National Economic University. However, he never worked in his field of specialization.

1997: As a member of the Zaporizhzhya–Kryvyi Rih– Transit team, Zelensky became champion in the *KVK* Premier League on Russian television. Subsequently, the Kvartal 95 comedy team was created with Zelensky as its frontman; it competed in the *KVK* until 2003.

May 31, 1997: Borys Yeltsin and Leonid Kuchma signed the Treaty on Cooperation and Partnership between Russia and Ukraine. The document declared, among other things, the inviolability of the countries' existing borders and respect for territorial integrity.

2003: Volodymyr Zelensky became co-owner and art director of the Kvartal 95 Studio.

November 2004: Following the second round of the presidential election, the Central Election Commission declared Viktor Yanukovych the winner. Supporters of his opponent, Viktor Yushchenko, accused the authorities of election fraud and protested in the streets – this became known as the Orange Revolution. The Supreme Court decided to hold a second round of elections, and Yushchenko was declared the winner.

2005: Kvartal 95 Studio produced the satirical comedy show *Vechirniy Kvartal* (*Evening Kvartal*), in which Volodymyr Zelensky was one of the main stars.

January 17, 2010: Viktor Yanukovych won the presidential election.

2010–12: Zelensky served as general producer of the Inter TV channel.

November 2013: Citizens dissatisfied with Yanukovych's rejection of Ukraine's integration with Europe gathered on the Maidan (Independence Square) in Kyiv. This escalated into the Revolution of Dignity, which ended with Yanukovych fleeing to Russia.

February 20, 2014: The annexation of Crimea by Russia began.

February 23, 2014: Oleksandr Turchynov became acting president of Ukraine.

April 2014: Russians and Russian-backed separatists occupied Slovyansk, Kramatorsk, and Druzhkivka: the war in the Donbas began.

April 17, 2014: A meeting was held in Geneva between top diplomatic envoys from Ukraine, Russia, the USA, and the EU. The aim was to resolve the armed conflict between Russia and Ukraine. The participants agreed on the disarmament of all illegal military groups; on the return to their lawful owners of all illegally seized buildings; on the liberation of all illegally seized streets, squares, and other public places in cities and towns. All protesters and those who vacated buildings and other public places and voluntarily laid down their arms were guaranteed amnesty, except for those who were found guilty of serious crimes.

May 25, 2014: Petro Poroshenko was elected president of Ukraine.

September 5, 2014: Representatives of Ukraine, the Organization for Security and Cooperation in Europe (OSCE), and Russia signed the Minsk Protocol (Minsk-1), an agreement to a ceasefire in the war in eastern Ukraine. The leaders of the self-proclaimed "People's Republics" of LPR and DPR also signed the protocol. Two weeks later, the parties agreed to a withdrawal of troops from the border, the establishment of a 30-kilometer safety zone, and the withdrawal of heavy weapons.

February 11–12, 2015: The leaders of Germany, France, Ukraine, and Russia agreed on a package of measures to implement the Minsk agreements in order to de-escalate the armed conflict in eastern Ukraine. This document, Minsk-2, was signed by representatives from Ukraine, Russia, and the self-proclaimed "People's Republics" of LPR and DPR. Agreements relating to the Donetsk and Luhansk regions included: the right to hold elections, approval of legislation on the special status of certain isolated districts, amnesty for some of those involved in events that took place in certain areas, withdrawal of foreign troops and restoration of Ukrainian control over the Ukrainian–Russian border.

2015–18: In the TV series *Servant of the People* Volodymyr Zelensky played the role of history teacher Vasyl Holoborodko, who was elected president.

2017: Ukraine's ministry of justice registered the Servant of the People Party (Sluha Narodu).

December 31, 2018: Volodymyr Zelensky announced he would run for the presidency.

April 21, 2019: Volodymyr Zelensky was elected president of Ukraine.

July 2019: The Servant of the People Party won a majority in the parliamentary elections.

July 2019: Volodymyr Zelensky held a phone conversation with the US President Donald Trump. Two months later, Trump was accused of putting pressure on Zelensky over the investigation into Joe Biden's son Hunter, whom Trump alleged had engaged in corrupt activities in Ukraine. On **December 19, 2019** the US House of Representatives voted to impeach Trump. The US Senate acquitted him on **February 13, 2020**.

December 9, 2019: The Normandy Format meeting was held at the Élysée Palace in Paris between the Ukrainian President Volodymyr Zelensky, Russian President Vladimir Putin, French President Emmanuel Macron, and German Chancellor Angela Merkel. The meeting was the first and last one-on-one private conversation between Putin and Zelensky. The Normandy Four agreed on a partial withdrawal of forces in the Donbas at three checkpoints, a complete ceasefire until December 31, 2019, and a follow-up meeting of the Four in spring 2020.

February 2, 2021: The National Security and Defense Council of Ukraine decided to impose sanctions against people's deputy Taras Kozak and the TV channels 112 Ukraine, NewsOne, and ZIK, owned by Viktor Medvedchuk, who is godfather to one of Putin's children. The head of the Security Service of Ukraine, Ivan Bakanov, called the decision of the RNBO "a consistent step taken by the Ukrainian authorities to combat Russian hybrid aggression."

2021: Viktor Medvedchuk was accused of committing treason, of assisting a terrorist organization, and attempting to plunder national resources in the temporarily occupied territory of Crimea in Ukraine. In May 2021, he was put under house arrest. However, just after the outbreak of war, Medvedchuk escaped, but, on **April 12, 2022**, he was arrested by the Ukrainian secret service.

February 21, 2022: Russian President Vladimir Putin signed decrees recognizing the "independence" of the DPR and LPR.

February 24, 2022: Russia launched a full-scale military invasion of Ukraine.

May 3, 2022: The Verkhovna Rada made the decision to ban the activities of pro-Russian parties in Ukraine. The ban applies to those political actors who publicly deny Russia's armed aggression against Ukraine and annexation of Ukrainian territories, and who justify Putin's violation of Ukraine's territorial integrity and sovereignty.

CPSIA information can be obtained
at www.ICGtesting.com
Printed in the USA
BVHW032033160722
642123BV00006B/17/J